Day by Day with God

ROOTING WOMEN'S LIVES IN THE BIBLE

SEPTEMBER–DECEMBER 2005

Christina Press
BRF
Tunbridge Wells/Oxford

The Bible Reading Fellowship,
First Floor, Elsfield Hall, 15–17 Elsfield Way, Oxford OX2 8FG

First published in Great Britain 2005

ISBN 1 84101 273 4

Distributed in Australia by:
Willow Connection, PO Box 288, Brookvale, NSW 2100.
Tel: 02 9948 3957; Fax: 02 9948 8153;
E-mail: info@willowconnection.com.au

Distributed in New Zealand by:
Scripture Union Wholesale, PO Box 760, Wellington
Tel: 04 385 0421; Fax: 04 384 3990; E-mail:
suwholesale@clear.net.nz

Acknowledgments

Scripture quotations taken from The Holy Bible, New International
Version, copyright © 1973, 1978, 1984 by International Bible
Society. Used by permission of Hodder & Stoughton Ltd. All rights
reserved. 'NIV' is a registered trademark of International Bible
Society. UK trademark number 1448790.

Scriptures from The New Revised Standard Version of the Bible,
Anglicized Edition, copyright © 1989, 1995 by the Division of
Christian Education of the National Council of the Churches of
Christ in the USA, used by permission. All rights reserved.

Scripture quotations from the Contemporary English Version ©
American Bible Society 1991, 1992, 1995. Used by
permission/Anglicizations © Britih and Foreign Bible Society
1997.

Scripture quotations reprinted from The New Testament in
Modern English, Revised Edition, translated by J.B. Phillips.
Published by HarperCollins Publishers Ltd.

Scripture quotations marked (NLT) are taken from the Holy Bible,
New Living Translation, copyright © 1996. Used by permission of
Tyndale House Publishers, Inc., Wheaton, Illinois 60189. All
rights reserved.

Scripture quotations from THE MESSAGE. Copyright © by Eugene
H. Peterson 1993, 1994, 1995. Used by permission of NavPress
Publishing Group.

'The power of your love' by Geoff Bullock. Copyright © 1992
Maranatha!Music/Word Music Inc. Administered by CopyCare,
PO Box 77, Hailsham, BN27 3EF, UK. music@copycare.com.
Used by permission.

Printed in Great Britain by Bookmarque, Croydon

Contents

Contributors

Heather Coupland enjoys sharing in full-time ministry with her husband Simon, who is a vicar in Kingston-Upon-Thames. As well as doing some freelance writing, she loves cooking, reading and walking in Richmond Park with her daughter Pippa.

Diana Archer is a writer, mum of three, and wife of Graham, Anglican vicar in Southampton. She has been managing editor of *Connect* Bible studies, and wrote *Who'd Plant a Church*, a warts-and-all account of church planting in the UK.

Rosemary Green is a wife, mother and grandmother of twelve. She has varied experience in Christian ministry and loves encouraging Christians in their growth in Bible knowledge, prayer and Christian service.

Margaret Killingray works for the London Institute for Contemporary Christianity in central London, where she teaches and writes a weekly email Bible message. She is married to David, and has three married daughters and seven grandchildren.

Celia Bowring (CB) and husband Lyndon have three children and work with CARE. Celia compiles CARE's *Prayer Guide* and is writing a book about 'Living with Leadership', a national network which she coordinates, encouraging ministers' wives.

Anne Coomes is a writer and editor of www.parishpump.co.uk, a website for church magazine editors. She also edits *Decision* magazine (UK edition) for the Billy Graham Evangelistic Association and Samaritan's Purse.

Catherine Butcher (CFB) is editor of *Day by Day with God*. A freelance writer and a regular contributor to *Christianity*, she lives in Sussex with her family where she enjoys walking, watercolour painting, swimming and reading.

Bridget Plass has a gift of seeing Jesus in the ordinary messiness of real life. She has written a Lent book, *Challenges of the Narrow Way*, and leads occasional Quiet Days for BRF.

Wendy Bray is an award-winning writer and journalist. A cancer survivor, she has an interest in faith, life and survivorship issues and runs 'One Life', a personal development and life coaching initiative.

The Editor writes...

If you've been reading through this series throughout the year, you will know that we have been following the theme of God's rescue plan: how God created men and women with all we needed for abundant life—creative, fulfilling work; a beautiful place to live; companionship and communion with each other and with himself; abundant provision; boundaries to keep us safe; and hope for a future in harmony with our heavenly Father. We began by looking at the perfect harmony of the Trinity, then Satan's fall from heaven and the spoilt potential of Eden. Aloneness, separation from God and banishment from home are themes which have recurred through the year as we have looked at God's plan to bring people back into relationship with himself.

Even if you have not been following the notes through the whole year, you will find invaluable insights as you dig into the Bible in the next four months. We will be looking in particular at Jesus—the embodiment of God's amazing love, the one who makes us whole and gives us identity, security and an eternal home. The aim of these notes is to help us to grasp the big picture of God's plan for human history. From that perspective we will be better equipped to share our faith with our contemporaries, many of whom have lost the plot and can only see life's brokenness, futility and unmet needs, rather than God's love, purpose and protection.

You will find a Bible reading for each day; aim to read it all rather than just the verse quoted at the top of the notes. Ask God to speak to you personally from his word and take note of any thoughts or impressions that occur to you as you read the scripture passage for the day. The notes are written to help you as you seek to root your life in the Bible, but don't just rely on the notes. Expect God to give you insights that touch precisely on the issues you are facing. Something supernatural takes place when people allow God to speak to them through scripture. The Holy Spirit does what Jesus promised: 'when he, the Spirit of truth, comes, he will guide you into all truth' (John 16:13).

Allow God to speak to you and let his words take root in your life, bearing fruit in faith, hope and love for God and the people who cross your path.

Catherine Butcher

Watch and learn

Jesus gave them this answer: 'I tell you the truth, the Son can do nothing by himself; he can do only what he sees his Father doing, because whatever the Father does the Son also does.'

Have you ever watched a child copying a parent as they master some new skill? Maybe you've seen a toddler on the beach endeavouring to make a sandcastle as beautiful as the one Mum or Dad so effortlessly produced! I have loved cooking since I was a little girl. I can still remember standing alongside my mother in our kitchen as with end-less patience she taught me some new technique such as rolling out pastry or separating an egg! I couldn't have succeeded without watching her carefully and then doing it for myself. This is how we learn as human beings and as Christians too.

Jesus states he could do nothing by himself. *The Message* translation says, 'The Son can't independently do a thing' (v. 19). There is a difference here between my learning process in the kitchen and Jesus with his Father. My mother rightly wanted me to become independent of her as I learnt to do things on my own. Jesus' attitude shows us that we need to become more and more dependent on our heavenly Father; not learning and moving away, but learning and staying alongside.

Being dependent on something is often seen as negative in our society, but we have to learn to think in a different way. I love J.B. Phillips' translation of Romans 12:2: 'Don't let the world squeeze you into its mould'. The world says self-sufficiency is best. The Word says depend on God.

As the summer holidays draw to a close we're going to be looking at the theme of 'Back to work' specifically considering how we use our time in the light of Jesus' example to us. Are we dependent on him as we plan our time or do we have our own independent agenda?

....

Ask God now to help you to be aware of him in everything you do today and dependent on him in every situation, just as Jesus was.

HC

A purposeful life

Immediately Jesus made his disciples get into the boat and go ahead of him… *Immediately* he spoke to them and said, 'Take courage! It is I. Don't be afraid.'… *As soon as* they got out of the boat, people recognized Jesus.

I have to confess that just sitting down to read Mark's Gospel makes me feel tired! Jesus strides purposefully from one action-packed incident to the next. Calling disciples, driving out demons, healing, teaching, calming storms—it's all a bit overwhelming! How does he do it? What vitamin supplement does he take?

It seems to me that Jesus' life was a life in perfect balance. Whatever he did, he did purposefully and calmly. He was constantly busy and in demand and yet reading through the Gospels you don't sense any panic in Jesus because of the pressure he's under. This must surely have been because a) he was in constant communication with his Father, and b) he understood and accepted his mission on earth. He knew where his focus should be. Do we?

My husband is a vicar and when we arrived in one of our parishes I spread myself too thinly for a while by becoming involved in too much. Consequently I didn't do any particular thing to the best of my ability and felt frustrated. As time goes by I am learning to be more discerning and to use my time for the things God lays on my heart and not on what I feel a perfect vicar's wife 'should' be doing!

The start of a new academic year is a good opportunity to take stock of our lives and how we use our time. Do we have a sense of God leading us and giving a sense of purpose? God chose each one of us to be his children and to fulfil a unique task for him (Ephesians 2:10). Are we on a treadmill that is exhausting and going nowhere; or are we in tune with God, stepping out beside him fulfilling his purpose for our lives?

....

Hold your diary/calendar open before God and ask him to show you his priorities for your life. Are any changes needed?

Try reading through Mark's Gospel in one sitting to see how purposeful Jesus was in all he said and did.

HC

Time for God

Yet the news about him spread all the more, so that crowds of people came to hear him and to be healed of their sicknesses. But Jesus often withdrew to lonely places and prayed.

Yesterday we saw that although Jesus was busy he lived his life purposefully. He knew his priorities and one of them was to withdraw 'as often as possible' (v. 16, *The Message*) to have time with his Father. I find it hard during the summer holidays to keep to any pattern of Bible reading so September is a good time for a fresh start as my daughter goes back to school and new routines begin.

Whether we live by ourselves or in a family, work full-time, are unemployed or retired, somehow it's never easy to carve out time to spend on our own with God. It was a struggle for Jesus too! Time and again he tries to be on his own or just with his disciples but these efforts are thwarted as people follow them around. Sometimes Jesus has compassion and ministers to the people's needs (Matthew 14:14), but sometimes he sees the crowd and chooses to 'cross to the other side of the lake' (Matthew 8:18). It's all a question of priorities.

In my quest to find the perfect 'Quiet Time' I have tried getting up early and going to bed extra late. I have tried using lunchtimes, coffee breaks and have gone for walks. I have fasted in order to pray and I have feasted on gourmet fare at weekends away on retreat…

It is important to be kind to ourselves and realize that what suits one person doesn't necessarily work for someone else and that at each different stage in our lives we need to be adaptable and creative. In other words, there is no 'one size fits all' relationship with God! Let's feel free to experiment and recognize that the issue is less about when or how we spend time with God, and more about whether we make it a priority or not.

....

Lord, I long to get to know you better and to hear you speaking to me each day. Help me to make time for our relationship to grow.

                                                                                    HC

Time out!

Then, because so many people were coming and going that they did not even have a chance to eat, he said to them, 'Come with me by yourselves to a quiet place and get some rest.'

I wonder how good you are at taking time off. Do you feel guilty at the thought of taking some time out just to have a rest? Jesus didn't! He sometimes slipped away by himself and here we see him trying to get the disciples away from the crowds so they could all have a rest together. If we want to learn to imitate what Jesus did, we must learn the importance of simply taking time for rest and relaxation. Sometimes we wrongly equate busyness with success when we should be looking for a life in balance as the right way to live.

My husband and I have the same day off each week. He is very good at switching off with a cup of coffee and the newspaper and not involving himself in any work-related tasks. I, on the other hand am tempted to use the time to catch up with housework and errands. The trouble is that it then doesn't feel like time off and I end up feeling rather cheated and resentful. Inevitably there will be times when we have to catch up with things, but let's take every opportunity we can to take some time to chill out and relax. As women, many of us find this very difficult and guilt is our constant companion if we do decide to sit down with a cuppa when we could be doing something more 'productive'.

I believe passionately that rest is a good use of our time. It is both productive and restorative. I think Jesus thought so too. He didn't say: 'Come to me all you who are weary and burdened and I will give you a guilty conscience because what you have done still isn't enough.' He said he wanted to give us *rest*. Will we let him?

....

Give yourself permission today to 'rest' in whatever way appeals to you, and be aware of God reaching out to bless you.

Read Psalm 23 to see how God wants to lead you to rest as well as to work.

HC

9

Opportunity knocks

Be very careful, then, how you live—not as unwise but as wise, making the most of every opportunity.

I confess that I am a serial list-maker! And, yes, I have been known to write something on my 'to do' list that I have already done, just to have the satisfaction of crossing it off! Lists focus the mind on what needs to be done and give you a great boost when things are completed. But becoming a slave to your list does have its drawbacks. What about when you need to abandon the list because your child/husband/friend needs a hug and a listening ear? What about writing a note of encouragement to someone God has placed on your heart or spending extra time in prayer for a particular person or situation? Are we flexible enough with our time to listen to what God wants us to do, even if at the end of the day nothing is crossed off our list?

I know that some of us can be more flexible with our days than others, but all our time is a gift from God and we need to learn to use it wisely. Even if we work full-time, certain aspects of our time within the working environment and at home are still within our control.

I love the phrase in this passage, 'making the most of every opportunity' because it sounds as if the way I use my time can be both exciting and significant. Sometimes it's easy to see 'time' as an enemy. We talk of 'fighting against the clock', and our 'to do' lists can become burdens on our backs rather than tools to help us. Each day God gives us choices in the way we use our time and our attitude to it. Even if we know today is going to be hectic, let's make the most of every minute we are given!

....

Lord, please help me today to see my time as a gift from you. Help me to 'make the most of every opportunity' to use my time for your glory.

HC

Working at waiting!

Yet when he heard that Lazarus was sick, he stayed where he was two more days.

We have seen already that Jesus knew when to act and when to withdraw. He also knew when to wait. Most of us find waiting hard work and tend to consider any time spent waiting as rather a waste. Waiting can be stressful as it makes us late for the next activity in our busy schedule. Waiting can cause blood pressure to rise and patience to slip away.

Jesus' example in today's reading shows us how, on hearing of a friend's serious illness, he made the deliberate decision to wait (v. 6). This seems harsh to us, but commentators on this passage believe that Jesus was resolutely refusing to be manipulated (see also 2:4; 7:3–6) because he was waiting for his Father's perfect timing. This resulted in bringing greater glory to God and a life-changing revelation of the power of God to the people present.

Before my husband began his present job we had a period of waiting. During this time God reminded me of the line in a song: 'and as I wait I'll rise up like the eagle, and I will soar with you, your spirit leads me on in the power of your love'. Those words put waiting in a new light for me. Waiting doesn't have to be pointless and frustrating but can be fruitful and purposeful as we listen to God and keep in step with him.

At this time of year as we think of our theme of 'Back to work' with respect to our time, it can feel as if we should be planning more things to do and trying to fit in more than ever. Are we rushing into something that needs some more thought or making decisions too quickly? Do we need to 'wait' before the Lord to hear what he has to say?

....

Are you waiting for something in your life at the moment? Surrender whatever it is to God's timing and will today.

Read Isaiah 8:17, 26:8, 30:18 and 64:4 to see how the people had to learn to wait and were blessed when they did.

HC

The right time

Therefore Jesus told them, 'The right time for me has not yet come… You go to the Feast. I am not yet going up to this Feast, because for me the right time has not yet come.' Having said this, he stayed in Galilee.

Here we have another example of Jesus understanding when to act and when to wait. Have you noticed how our opinion about when a certain thing should happen and God's attitude to that same thing are often completely different?

As I write this I have just returned from a trip to Morocco visiting one of our church's mission partners. I have been wanting to go ever since I heard about the work there, eight years ago, but the time never seemed quite 'right' until now. The crazy thing is that my husband and I are about to take up a job in a new church. From a human perspective this timing seems all wrong. Had I gone five years ago, there would have been plenty of time to encourage others to visit mission partners and really 'fly the flag' for these amazing people who go out from our churches. I might even have had time to visit more than once, providing ongoing support.

In Greek there are two different words for time. One is *chronos*, meaning literally the time of day (from which we get our word 'chronology'). The other is *kairos*, which has much more to do with a particular point in time or opportune moment (Mark 1:15).

In our passage today Jesus' brothers are advising him on the best strategy for him to become a public figure. It is logical to them that now is the time to show himself to the world by performing miracles in a more public arena. For Jesus, however, now is not the time.

I might never understand why I went to Morocco when I did, but that's not really the issue. I went in obedience to what I felt God was saying, and had a life-changing trip!

....

Lord, I don't always understand your timing. Help me to trust you and to experience your peace when I get confused.

Read Ecclesiastes 3:1–11 for an Old Testament perspective on 'the right time'.

HC

Out of control!

Peter got down out of the boat, walked on the water and came towards Jesus. But when he saw the wind, he was afraid and, beginning to sink, cried out, 'Lord, save me!' Immediately Jesus reached out his hand and caught him. 'You of little faith,' he said, 'why did you doubt?'

Most of us like to have some sense of being in control. Choosing how we use our time is one way we can bring some order into our often chaotic lives.

A while ago my husband suffered a detached retina. For two weeks he had to lie face down and was only allowed to be upright for ten minutes in every hour. At first I was determined to be the model wife/nurse/carer, but the novelty soon wore off. I felt terrible about being in such a bad mood when it wasn't even me who was suffering. 'Why am I feeling so awful?' I moaned to God. Immediately the words came to my mind, 'Is it because you're feeling out of control?' I gulped. Yes, that was exactly it.

Peter was full of good intentions. We don't know how he was feeling inside, but he wanted with all his heart to be obedient to Jesus, as long as the wind was still and the water was calm!

In Jesus' ministry it sometimes may have looked as if things were getting out of control: people wanting to manipulate him, crowds physically pushing him around. We don't know whether Jesus ever felt that awful panicky sensation that can result in situations like these, but we can be sure that he trusted his Father in any and every circumstance. That trust ultimately enabled him to die on the cross for you and me.

I believe God wanted to teach me that being out of control isn't the end of the world. Life isn't predictable and we need to learn to cope with the unexpected and undesirable by acknowledging he is there for us, whatever else is going on around us.

....

Are there areas of your life that feel out of control? Give them to God and trust him to understand, and carry you through.

Read 2 Corinthians 6:1–10 to see how out of control Paul's life was, yet how fruitful.

HC

Living in the light of eternity

For God so loved the world that he gave his one and only Son, that whoever believes in him shall not perish but have eternal life.

I clearly remember a friend of mine grasping the concept of eternal life for the very first time as she read Jesus' words in John 8:51: 'whoever keeps my word will never see death'. She spent the rest of the day rushing around saying to everyone, 'I'm not going to see death, I'm not going to see death.' She had suddenly realized her eternal life had already begun. She had 'crossed over from death to life' (John 5:24), and couldn't keep quiet about it.

Some people view our time on earth as a time of waiting before the real action begins. Some see it as a place where we sit examinations to see whether we will graduate or not. For others it is like a dress rehearsal before the big performance. But none of these views really does justice to what the Bible portrays. Our mortal existence isn't just a means to an end; it is much more significant than that. Eternal life, as my friend had seen, is not a replacement for life on earth but the continuation of a life already begun in heaven, which has infinite meaning and importance.

What we do with our time here has consequences for ourselves and for those around us. It is sobering to think that the way I treat my neighbour could have consequences in eternity. Will my attitudes and actions put them off Jesus or attract them to him?

Jesus lived his life in the knowledge of his own impending death but then of eternal glory beside his Father. He didn't sit back thinking it would work out all right in the end. He served, he healed, he loved and even in death he forgave, reaping for us life with him for ever.

....

Lord, help me to live today in the light of eternity, to be aware that what I say and do can have consequences in other people's lives.

HC

Time as a gift

But I trust in you, O Lord; I say, 'You are my God.' My times are in your hands.

Whether we are in a situation where we feel we never have a spare minute or whether we feel time lying heavy on our hands, each 24 hours is a precious gift from God. We may not think we have much choice in how we use our time because of circumstances, but each of us is responsible for our attitude to the time we have been given.

In today's Bible reading the psalmist starts by pleading with God for deliverance from his enemies. He asks God to listen to him and save him because of his great distress. He is ill and anxious and, up until verse 13, things seem to be getting steadily worse!

Then in verse 14 we read this wonderful declaration of trust in God and the tone of the psalm begins to change. Instead of bitter complaint we hear a new confidence in the requests (vv. 16–18). The final section is full of praise to God for his love and help.

The psalmist's physical situation probably didn't change during the writing of these verses but his attitude to it did. That change in outlook was what seemed to make all the difference.

I may not be surrounded by enemies and 'consumed with anguish' (v. 10) in the same way the psalmist was, but life can be pretty awful sometimes. When friends hurt us or our health fails, depression can easily take hold and misery can become a pattern from which it is hard to escape.

Whatever our situation at the moment, let's resolve to declare our trust in God even when the going is tough. Let's give every minute he has given us back to him and ask him to teach us afresh how to use the gift of time to his glory.

....

Take a few moments to memorize verses 14 and 15 and make a decision to give your time back to God instead of taking it into your own hands.

HC

To glorify God...

In John 17 we have a unique insight into Jesus' prayer life as John records Jesus' prayer for the disciples and for us who believe in Jesus because of their message. Throughout the prayer, Jesus' priority is that God should receive glory. When 17th-century Christians in Westminster were trying to summarize our goal in life they concluded that our primary purpose is to glorify God, and to enjoy him forever (*Westminster Shorter Catechism*, 1647). Does that purpose statement describe your last two weeks? Has God's glory been your first priority? Have you been enjoying your relationship with him?

Jesus does not set us an impossible task. As he said in his prayer, he gives us *his* glory. We don't have to work at achieving some impossible standard. Jesus has done all the work. He has made the ultimate sacrifice. His glory is seen when we trust him in difficult circumstances, set aside our own priorities to serve others, and obey him in the way we behave, with honesty, integrity and goodness. At the start of his ministry, Jesus used Isaiah 61:1–3 as his purpose statement:

'The Spirit of God, the Master, is on me because God anointed me. He sent me to preach good news to the poor, heal the heartbroken, announce freedom to all captives, pardon all prisoners. God sent me to announce the year of his grace—a celebration of God's destruction of our enemies—and to comfort all who mourn, to care for the needs of all who mourn in Zion, give them bouquets of roses instead of ashes, messages of joy instead of news of doom, a praising heart instead of a languid spirit. Rename them "Oaks of Righteousness" planted by God to display his glory.' (*THE MESSAGE*)

These words describe our rescuer's strategy. Over the next two weeks, Diana Archer will be looking at Jesus, the rescuer; our hero. At first glance, Jesus isn't like the rescuer or hero of childhood adventure stories. But like many great heroes he is in the business of defeating enemies and giving 'bouquets of roses'; setting captives free. And, true to the image of a heroic rescuer, he risks everything for love.

He's my hero!

So the three mighty men broke through the Philistine lines, drew water from the well near the gate of Bethlehem and carried it back to David. But he refused to drink it; instead he poured it out before the Lord.

Who is your hero? Is it someone you know personally or do thoughts of James Bond sweep irresistibly into your mind? 'The name's Bond. James Bond.' With these words, 007 defines himself as the popular image of a hero—clever, daring, and ready to take extraordinary risks to rescue ordinary people (as long as they are exceptionally pretty). Bond is also gorgeous, sensitive and charming, of course, depending on who is your favourite Bond actor.

David's three mighty men strike me as early Israelite James Bond characters. Out of love and loyalty to their commander David, they broke through enemy lines just to get him a drink of water from the Bethlehem well. Locked in vicious combat with the Philistines, David is overwhelmed by their daring actions and gives their gift the highest honour by offering it to God. More powerful exploits of these three—and indeed the Thirty Mighty Men as well—are recorded in the rest of the chapter. It's all high-action, swash-buckling stuff. It would probably get an '18' film rating. Although Josheb-Basshebeth, Eleazar and Shammah may not be as easy to say as James…

Judging by these standards then, was—is—Jesus a hero? He was born a nobody in a minor district of the Roman empire. His life attracted no attention before he was 30-something. He didn't lead an army or become known for his physical prowess. He wasn't married. He looked pretty normal. He didn't challenge the occupying forces to a duel. He walked about the place. He said a lot.

Yet people followed Jesus. And still do.

....

Why do you follow him?

DA

An alternative hero

Pilate… had Jesus flogged, and handed him over to be crucified. The soldiers… twisted together a crown of thorns and set it on him… Again and again they struck him on the head with a staff and spat on him.

Have you seen the film *The Passion of the Christ* produced by Mel Gibson? It caused some interesting ructions among my Christian friends, some of whom refused to see it because of the reputed violence, and some who wanted to show it to everyone. Yes, I did go, partly because I was fascinated that a film recorded entirely in Aramaic and Latin could cause such a wonderful stir. And yes, it was unforgettable. The violence was gruelling, though not really anything worse than scenes I have pictured in my head every Easter for years. We know the Easter story. We know Jesus didn't look like your average hero as he stumbled towards one of the cruellest deaths ever invented.

The film spared no detail of a Roman flogging. Jesus' body was literally mashed by the whips, front and back. Then he still had to get his cross and himself outside the city to the place of crucifixion. Huge nails were waiting to pinion him to the wood. Hero? Not by Bond standards. But then Bond never endured the same level of suffering. The fact that Jesus could still walk after the beating was amazing enough, and was really brought home to me by seeing it on the screen.

What sort of hero is Jesus? He is the sort who faces explicit suffering with courage and strength. Not for him the last-minute escape from danger from whence the hero emerges with his hair unruffled. Jesus went to the end of the line for you and for me. He did the death bit. He redefined the word 'hero' as something the world can never match.

....

How much is Jesus your hero?   See Luke 4:23–30 for an example of Jesus' strength of character.

DA

A hero's perspective

'Father, if you are willing, take this cup from me; yet not my will but yours be done'... And being in anguish, he prayed more earnestly, and his sweat was like drops of blood falling to the ground.

Yes, I know it's not very chronological to have Jesus in Gethsemane after we have already looked at his crucifixion, but bear with me. What sort of hero is Jesus? Why did he do what he did? Surely this prayer in the garden was a hugely defining moment. This was the real battle. It was here that Jesus chose to stick to his Father's plan, no matter what it cost him.

A couple of days ago, I asked who is your hero? If you managed to resist screen idols, I suspect the person you thought of was someone who helps you out when you really need it, or who embodies the type of person you would like to be. You respond to the values your hero lives by, and have benefited from them. There's something about our heroes—whether male or female—that inspires us.

My hero? I have lots actually. There's the woman who ignited my hunger for God, by demonstrating her own. She then gave me oodles of time and helped me untangle the knots in my head. There's my friend who lives with muscular dystrophy and refuses to let it dominate her life. There's a chap who went to dangerous countries on behalf of Tear Fund, the Christian relief charity. And his wife, who let him go. I think most pastors are heroes too, though I may be biased here.

Genuine heroes live by principles that challenge the easy way out. They are 'big picture' people who refuse to give in. They care about others. Like Jesus, they face horrendous situations with courage. Like Jesus, it takes a lot of battling through anguish. Like Jesus, 'thy will be done' turns out to be a costly prayer.

Perhaps that is why they are my heroes. They are indeed like Jesus.

Dear Lord, help me to learn more about the values you lived by. Help me to see the 'big picture' when the challenges of life threaten to overwhelm me. Help me to pray 'Your will be done' when I need to.

DA

Why did he do it?

'As the Father has loved me, so have I loved you. Now remain in my
love... My command is this: Love each other as I have loved you.
Greater love has no one than this, to lay down one's life for one's
friends.'

It is all about love. The reason Jesus came to be a hero was because
of love. It wasn't because he had something to prove, or wanted people to think he was great. It wasn't because his death would advance
the political cause of the Jews against the occupying Roman forces.
It wasn't because he wanted to be a hero either. That just happened
anyway. It was because of love.

I am sure that many famous people are seduced by the thought of
making a name for themselves, whatever the reason for their fame. To
go down in the history books—isn't that a sort of immortality? To be
remembered for something amazing? A cut above the average? Why,
we can even be tempted to this in our Christian circles, although we
make it all sound very holy. We just want to count for something.

I am not saying this is all wrong, just that it is a million miles away
from where Jesus started. He came from a relationship of love with
his Father and acted out of love all the time. This was his motivation.
His extraordinary security as a human being was based purely in
love. He received it and he gave it. Every interaction with the people
he met was bathed in it. He healed because he loved. He taught
because he loved. He challenged because he loved. He went to the
cross because he loved. He was 1 Corinthians 13 before Paul ever
wrote it. That's why he came to rescue us.

Now Jesus invites us into that same love. As *The Message* puts it
'Make yourselves at home in my love. If you keep my commands,
you'll remain intimately at home in my love.'

....

Take some time today to make   Read 1 Corinthians 13.
sure you are at home in God's   DA
love.

Responding to love

'This woman… wet my feet with her tears and wiped them with her hair… this woman… has not stopped kissing my feet… has poured perfume on my feet. Therefore, I tell you, her many sins have been forgiven—for she loved much.'

How do you respond to Jesus' love? Can you identify with the extravagant gestures of this woman?

Sometimes I think I am only at the very beginning of the beginning of understanding God's love for me. Having written down the challenge yesterday to 'remain' in Jesus' love, I wonder just how much at home I make myself. For example, how would I have reacted to 'this woman', if I had been around at that famous dinner in Simon the Pharisee's house? Picture the scene: Simon and his friends lounging around the low table, intrigued enough by this trouble-causing rabbi to invite him to a meal, but careful not to show him respect. Indeed, they weren't even bothered about offering him the common courtesies of footwashing, anointing his head with oil or the welcome kiss. Then along comes this infamous woman, who proceeds to horrify Simon by her attentions to his guest.

Would I, like Simon, simply judge both the woman and Jesus for this embarrassing display of emotion? Or would I be able to see the extraordinary truths of a forgiven woman responding in love and gratitude, and rejoice for her? Perhaps I would wish I had thought of it first—thought of finding a way to get close to Jesus and showing how I felt.

This woman's actions stemmed from a deep understanding of what Jesus had done for her. She knew that, against all the odds, this extraordinary rabbi had given her a new start. This was what Jesus came to do, then and now, for anyone who wanted it.

How would you have reacted to this incident, had you been there? What does your answer say about your relationship to Jesus, our hero and rescuer?

Read Song of Songs 4:9–10 and hear Jesus calling you, his beloved.

DA

The people's hero

Then Jesus asked them, 'Which is lawful on the Sabbath: to do good or to do evil, to save life or to kill?' But they remained silent. He looked round at them in anger and, deeply distressed at their stubborn hearts, said to the man, 'Stretch out your hand.' He stretched it out, and his hand was completely restored.

I have been thinking about other types of modern-day heroes. We are a strange species, the way we put people on pedestals. If you can get a ball into a net well, you're a hero. If you can sell a lot of films by acting in them, you are a celebrity. If you have loads of money and enjoy a privileged lifestyle, someone somewhere will want to photograph you. If you make music that people love, you are really hitting the hero stakes.

Why? Why are we so fascinated by the rich and the famous? Why are we blinded by status? Is it because, like the Pharisees in the story today, we want everything in recognizable order? We don't want someone who doesn't look like a hero coming along and upsetting the way we do things. We make our celebrities in our own image. We buy the newspapers and read the gossip columns.

What do you think Jesus would say about it all? Here in the synagogue, he did not hesitate to heal the man with the shrivelled hand, even though he knew he was making trouble for himself. The Pharisees were trying to catch out this man who challenged their way of doing things; Jesus' agenda was totally different. He was angered by their lack of compassion. Not just angry either, he was seriously unhappy. He took action immediately and showed his own compassion for the man by healing his hand. Jesus refused to play the popularity game. He didn't give a fig for his reputation. There were important principles at stake: like love, compassion, and knowing what God is really like.

....

On those days when you think God doesn't care about you, remember Jesus' reaction to uncaring attitudes.

Read John 6:14–15 to see what Jesus thought about pedestals.

DA

Action man

He made a whip out of cords, and drove all from the temple area, both sheep and cattle; he scattered the coins of the money-changers and overturned their tables. To those who sold doves he said, 'Get these out of here! How dare you turn my Father's house into a market!'

If you were invited to draw a picture of Jesus—supposing you could draw, which I can't—what would he look like? What pictures of Jesus do you have in your head that you might reproduce—any left over from childhood, or something more recent? Would your picture reflect something of his passion for his Father, as in this passage? I don't remember ever seeing a depiction of this scene in the temple, with a determined Jesus causing chaos. I do remember that one of Jesus standing on a hillock surrounded by cute animals.

While I am sure that Jesus has nothing against doves, in this tumultuous scene, he was only concerned that they were in the wrong place at the wrong time. He even took time to plait himself a whip to drive out the sheep. He turned over tables, upset people's livelihoods. He couldn't bear that the house of prayer had been turned into a jabbering marketplace. He did something about it.

No wonder the Jews asked him what authority he thought he had to do it. They must have been furious. Jesus, therefore, knew his actions were creating more antagonism from others, but that wasn't the point. He was a real hero, acting with passion and integrity, true to his calling.

It is not easy knowing that acting with integrity will invite opposition. We too are called to stand up for what is right, good and true, but others won't like it if it upsets the status quo. I am thinking of anything from fair trade to fair laws to fairness in relationships with family and friends.

....

Does God need you to be a hero in standing up for the good? What has he given you a passion for?

Read Isaiah 58:6–12 to discover God's priorities.

DA

23

True grit

He then began to teach them that the Son of Man must suffer many things and be rejected by the elders, chief priests and teachers of the law, and that he must be killed and after three days rise again... Peter took him aside and began to rebuke him.

To be honest, if I had been one of the disciples and heard Jesus start predicting his own betrayal, rejection and death, I think I would have been egging Peter on at this point. After all, being with Jesus was very exciting, what with miracles of healing and feeding, and amazing teaching that attracted vast crowds wherever Jesus went. The good news of the kingdom was very good indeed, and the disciples were at the centre of it! Why was Jesus bringing in all this bad news? Surely he was a match for anything that could threaten him—even the weather obeyed him (Luke 8:25).

I remember every Easter as a child hoping that the Good Friday story would end differently and that Jesus did not have to die this time. I imagine that Peter's rejection of Jesus' words was along similar lines. Of course we don't want the bad stuff; we don't want hard and difficult things to face. We want joy and glory, please, all the way to heaven. We really don't want to hear that suffering is going to be involved.

But true heroes refuse to give in to fear or denial. True heroes look squarely at the facts and find the courage to face them. Luke 9:51 tells us that Jesus 'resolutely set out for Jerusalem'. He takes Peter to task for speaking with the devil's temptation. Jesus stood against the fear in Peter's words, even though he knew how hard things would get. It wasn't easier for Jesus because he was God's Son. He had to find the grit and determination to go through with it. That's what true heroes do.

Thank you, Jesus, for being such a hero. Please help me when I face the bad stuff in my life. Give me your grit and determination.

See Psalm 143 for some empathy and encouragement.

DA

Against the odds

Then Satan entered Judas, called Iscariot, one of the Twelve. And Judas went to the chief priests and the officers of the temple guard and discussed with them how he might betray Jesus.

Have you ever been betrayed by a close friend? I expect most of us have been to one extent or another, and I think being betrayed is one of the hardest things to deal with. We've invested something of ourselves in a relationship or project; we've learned to trust and hope, and then the rug gets pulled out from under our feet. Whether it was conscious or not, someone has betrayed our trust and something very fundamental inside is badly damaged. The road to forgiveness and restoration is hard.

I guess it was even worse for Jesus. He knew it was going to happen. It is very interesting that Luke tells us Satan entered Judas. Despite having been outdone in the desert by Jesus (Luke 4:1–13), Satan had not given up. I don't know why Judas let him in, but we all have choices to make between good and evil. It meant that Jesus was really up against it: the chief priests were out for his hide, and so were the spiritual forces. A painful death was inevitable. How did Jesus keep being a hero in the middle of it all? He was betrayed by a close friend, and he faced the full force of evil head on, but he didn't flinch. He forgave and he kept his focus on what he was there to do.

It is so hard to go on when the odds against us seem overwhelming. But there are people who do it—people like missionaries, single parents, the seriously ill, survivors in famine-ravaged countries, the bereaved, victims of violence. You may know people who are having to be heroes at the moment. You may be one. Life can be tough. Can you take comfort and encouragement from the fact that Jesus *really* understands?

....

Dear Jesus, help me to appreciate what you went through for me. Show me what a difference that makes when I, or loved ones, go through tough times.

Read Hebrews 12:1–13 for some bracing realism!

DA

A hero's challenge

When they came to the place called the Skull, there they crucified him, along with the criminals—one on his right, the other on his left. Jesus said, 'Father, forgive them, for they do not know what they are doing.'

Every so often, incredible stories of forgiveness leak through the often cynical filter of the media. Suddenly, in the teeth of appalling tragedy, someone holds out forgiveness to the perpetrator of wrongdoing. I think of a story of a woman in South Africa who not only forgave the killer of her son, but adopted him into her family. Or a father in Northern Ireland who forgave when a bomb took the life of his daughter. Cutting through the never-ending cycles of hate and revenge, forgiveness is the only way out of humanity's spiral of violence.

But it is so difficult! I am in awe that Jesus could forgive his captors, even when they had just driven nails through his wrists. Presumably, he had already forgiven Judas. Jesus just doesn't stop being a hero. I feel ashamed that I struggle to forgive the silliest things, like a daughter who comes in late or my husband when he can't read my mind. But Jesus offered forgiveness at the moment of his greatest self-sacrifice. Not only was he devoid of self-seeking, but he was concerned for those who were mistreating him. While on the cross he also asked John to look after his mother and invited a criminal into paradise. No wonder the attendant centurion said, 'Surely this was a righteous man' (v. 47).

Jesus set a standard that is hard to reach without his help. I am convinced in my mind that forgiveness is non-negotiable for the Christian—'Keep us forgiven with you and forgiving others' (Matthew 6:15, *The Message*)—but my emotions are a problem. I know I will feel release when I manage to forgive, but I don't want to let go of my anger or sense of injustice. It's hard work to forgive and I usually need divine assistance. How about you?

....

Father, thank you for setting us free from guilt and condemnation.

Read Galatians 5:1. Don't miss out!

DA

SOS

The Spirit of the Sovereign Lord is on me, because the Lord has anointed me to preach good news to the poor. He has sent me to bind up the broken-hearted, to proclaim freedom for the captives and release from darkness for the prisoners, to proclaim the year of the Lord's favour.

Here we have Jesus' Hero Manifesto, which he announced to the synagogue in Nazareth (Luke 4:16). This is what he came to do. He never wavered from it and the Gospels resound with examples of him healing and releasing people physically, spiritually and emotionally. I hope you are convinced that Jesus qualifies for the greatest hero of all time.

But here comes the million-dollar question. Has he rescued you? Is he genuinely your hero? Perhaps you have prayed the prayer, believed in his sacrifice for you and given your life to him. Hallelujah! You gave the angels an excuse for a party. But how is it going now? We humans are strange beings. We have a fatal flaw that tempts us to take control of our own lives again, even after we have devoted them to God. It is so subtle, this drive, that half the time we don't realize we are doing it.

My vicar husband says the most requested song at the funerals of non-believers he takes is Frank Sinatra's 'I Did it My Way'. Doesn't that say something about our fierce drive for independence? Hard to rescue someone when they are insisting they can do it themselves. Being rescued involves dependence and helplessness, and those emotions don't come easy to homo sapiens.

As captives and prisoners we are not going to experience freedom unless we acknowledge the darkness we are in, and let Jesus get us out. This involves trust on our part, and a letting-go-of-control to God. It can be a struggle to do that, despite the fact our theology tells us that God has our best interests at heart, and loves us beyond measure. But we can't enjoy freedom until we are free.

....

How good are you at abandoning yourself to the love and rescue of God? Is there anything or anyone who could help you to 'let go'?

DA

27

Being rescued

'Our Father in heaven, hallowed be your name, your kingdom come, your will be done on earth as it is in heaven. Give us today our daily bread…'

I don't know how often you pray the Lord's Prayer, but we say it every week in our church. Although the words are so familiar, every so often I find that they suddenly strike me in a new way. Recently it has been the 'daily bread' bit. Although God is our all-time provider, Jesus told us to pray every day for our needs. It's that daily principle of throwing ourselves on God's mercy and trusting him to provide for us, in whatever way we need. It's an opportunity for daily rescue. It's depending and believing every day. Once, when I was struggling in a difficult situation, I told a friend, 'I don't understand it. I gave all this to God weeks ago!' She replied gently, 'Oh my dear. You have to give it to him every day.'

Which leads me on nicely to one of my favourite ways that God rescues us: through other people. Proverbs 17:17 says, 'A friend loves at all times, and a relative is born for adversity.' I have lost count of the many times I have been rescued by friends and family over the years. Friendship is a precious gift from God and he often works through our friends to reach us when we need it.

However, the same principle applies with our direct relationship with God: we need to be rescuable. We need to receive from others, we need to admit it when we need help, and we need to ditch our pride. None of us will be perfect this side of heaven, so why pretend? Why do we deprive our friends and family of the opportunity to help? Why do we deprive God of the same? How can Jesus be our daily hero unless we let him?

....

How much do you allow others to rescue you when you need it?

See Ecclesiastes 4:9–12 for the value of friendship.

DA

Being heroes

Whatever you do, do it all for the glory of God. Do not cause anyone to stumble, whether Jews, Greeks or the church of God—even as I try to please everybody in every way. For I am not seeking my own good but the good of many, so that they may be saved. Follow my example, as I follow the example of Christ.

Hands up those who could encourage others to imitate their lifestyle, with a clear conscience, like Paul does here. Personally I find the thought pretty alarming. I wouldn't really want anyone else duplicating the mess I often make of things. Paul's extraordinary confidence aside, what he really wants is for us to be like Jesus. When it comes to how we treat other people, he wants us to be heroes too.

So what about this helping others thing? Sometimes it can seem easier to give rather than receive, because it keeps us in the driving seat. Let's be honest—doing something helpful for someone else can make you feel good about yourself. That may not be entirely a bad thing, but I just can't imagine Jesus feeling a self-indulgent buzz every time he healed someone. I can, however, imagine him being joyful about it, delighted to bring more of God's kingdom on earth, and excited about the person's new start.

So the challenge is to bring our mixed, fallible motives to God and allow him to do a bit of purifying. I wonder if the secret is to offer anything we do for others to God first. Then he gets a gift from us, and we release the effects of our actions and love—and the glory—to him. A win-win situation. It might also make us more sensitive to how God wants to help: 'What would Jesus do?' As a general principle, I think that offering it all to God first could work. It would qualify for seeking the good of many, as Paul urges. It would focus our attention on God and others. I think it would be following Jesus' example.

....

Is it hard to think of yourself as a rescuer, or hero to anybody? See Ephesians 1:1–23 for the truth. You are loved. Find out what 'every spiritual blessing' means for you.

DA

A hero beyond words

His head and hair were white like wool… and his eyes were like blazing fire. His feet were like bronze glowing in the furnace… out of his mouth came a sharp double-edged sword. His face was like the sun shining in all its brilliance.

When John had this vision of Jesus, he 'fell at his feet as though dead'. Not surprising really. Any of us would have done the same. It seems John is struggling to find the words to describe what he saw—everything is 'like' something which doesn't quite do justice to it. There is no doubt, however, that whatever John saw, it was overwhelming. This is a big, big picture of Jesus. This is the hero revealed as he really is. As he says to John, 'Do not be afraid. I am the First and the Last' (v. 17). There is no one and nothing before or after him, or bigger or stronger. This is the Rescuer and Hero in all his truth and glory.

It is, of course, practically impossible for us to imagine what John saw. But I suspect that it is important for us to grasp something of its majesty and enormity. We need to know for sure that Jesus was not only a flesh-and-blood hero, but is also an eternal one who guarantees our future with him. Our security rests in his ultimate victory over evil. He is the hero who met the challenge and came out the winner. The qualities that make Jesus the greatest hero of all are part of him still, and are there for us to depend upon.

This is the Jesus we need whether life is good at the moment or difficult. It is the Jesus we need whether today is full of promise, scary, or just plain humdrum. When we are wrapped up in the everydayness of ordinary life, somewhere at the back of our minds we need a picture of Jesus that is big enough, loving enough and heroic enough to put our lives into perspective. We need an amazing Jesus who yet tells us not to be afraid.

....

What can you do today to help you to remember just how amazing Jesus is?

See Daniel 10:1–9 as a comparison with today's reading.

DA

Community focus

As Diana Archer pointed out a few days ago, one of the most popular songs chosen for funerals by non-Christians is Sinatra's 'I Did it My Way'. Here in the West we focus so much on individuals. As Christians it is easy to forget that the Bible is all about communities, and most of the New Testament is written to groups of believers. The only aspect of Eden that was 'not good' was Adam's solitude. God remedied that situation by giving him Eve, to complement him in every way (that's complement, as in make him complete—not compliment, as in boost his ego!).

God the Father, Son and Holy Spirit have always been in community and God does not intend for us to be alone. That's why his first task, after defeating death on the cross, was to give us his Holy Spirit, so we would never be alone. When Jesus became a man, he accepted the limits of time and space. But his Holy Spirit is not confined; he is always with us.

Jesus' next step was to build a community that could be his body on earth, showing the world what God is like. In the next two weeks Rosemary Green will be looking at Jesus' building process. How did he build the first church? What were its characteristics? What was its impact in first-century society?

Are you playing an active part in a community of believers? By becoming a Christian you have already become part of Christ's body, but God never intended you to function on your own. In our individualistic, pick and mix society, commitment through thick and thin isn't fashionable, even for churchgoers. People hop from church to church, looking for something that suits their needs—then they move on, when their need—or the church—changes.

According to Jean Vanier, leader of L'Arche community which includes many people with mental disabilities, it is the people we find hardest to like who are the ones who can help us most to grow.

'Let us not give up meeting together, as some are in the habit of doing, but let us encourage one another,' says the writer to the Hebrew (10:25). As we tackle our differences and work together, we show the world what the kingdom of God is like.

The birthday of the Church

There were staying in Jerusalem God-fearing Jews from every nation under heaven. When they heard this sound, a crowd came together in bewilderment, because each one heard them speaking in their own language. Utterly amazed, they asked: 'Are not all these who are speaking Galileans?... we hear them declaring the wonders of God in our own tongues!'

How many Christians do you know with a different racial background from your own? This scene in Jerusalem may seem a world away from our own lives. But try to imagine yourself out on the street when this group of 120 men and women appeared, speaking in the languages God had given them. You hear them praising God in English, but on your right is a woman who says in amazement, 'Ils parlent francais!' On your left is one who says, 'Sie sprechen Deutsch!' and beyond her, 'Oni mowia po Polsku!' How might you react?

It was no mistake that when the Holy Spirit came on the scene, Jerusalem was crowded. Residents in Jerusalem and visitors from the whole Middle East and eastern Mediterranean countries were together to celebrate the great Jewish Feast of Pentecost. Now they were going to hear good news about Jesus. During the next six weeks the risen Jesus met his followers many times; new understanding and new confidence began to grow, so that after his ascension they were content to wait prayerfully and expectantly for the next development.

In the next fortnight we will see how they began to grow into the worldwide Church we know today. It did not come easily. They met apathy, scepticism and violent opposition. Many Jewish Christians were reluctant to accept Gentiles on the basis only of their faith in Christ. Relationships were not always straightforward. But the cross, the resurrection and the Holy Spirit were all crucial in building their relationship with God and their relationships with one another.

....

Pray for the breakdown of barriers that exist between Christians of different backgrounds, despite Jesus' death which gives us all access to one Father.

Read Ephesians 2:13–22, verses that sum up our theme.

RG

The heart of the message

'You, with the help of wicked men, put him to death by nailing him to the cross. But God raised him from the dead, freeing him from the agony of death, because it was impossible for death to keep its hold on him.'

It was an amazing scene! Exultant disciples; an astonished crowd; some mockers. Peter stood up and preached a highly effective, off-the-cuff evangelistic sermon. He started where they were, with their accusations of drunkenness; he quoted scripture, and then moved on to speak about Jesus, crucified and risen, 'God has raised Jesus to life, and we are all witnesses of the fact.' He did not speak only about the most vital facts of Jesus' life; he spoke from his own firsthand experience. 'We know it's true, because we've seen him.'

The Holy Spirit gave Peter new freedom to speak out, very different from the Peter who denied even knowing Jesus during his trial. His boldness in speaking directly to his audience ('you, with the help of wicked men, put him to death') was matched by the directness of his call for response. 'Repent and be baptized' (v. 38). With that challenge came promises about what God would do for them and for us. 'You will be forgiven' (we should all be sure about that) and 'You will have God's Spirit in you.' We see the same clear message in 5:29–32 when the apostles were in front of the Jewish leaders.

Few of us are likely to be called on to do mass evangelism in the open air! But do we share Peter's freedom in talking about our faith, with neighbours, friends or colleagues? The strands we have seen in Peter's sermon are just as relevant for our personal conversations: linking into our friends' lives; understanding the heart of the gospel in Jesus' death and resurrection; giving testimony to our first-hand experience of the risen Lord; exercising the Spirit's gift of boldness; asking for a response; passing on God's promises; and using the Bible in support.

....

Lord, please help me to be secure in knowing what you have done for me and to be confident in sharing that faith with other people.

                                                                                              RG

Vibrant fellowship

They devoted themselves to the apostles' teaching and to the fellowship, to the breaking of bread and to prayer... They broke bread in
their homes and ate together with glad and sincere hearts, praising
God and enjoying the favour of all the people.

If you were to write a paragraph about the life of the church to which
you belong, what would you say? How would you convey its character?
How would it compare with the enthusiasm and joy of these first believers in Jerusalem? Notice some of the characteristics of their fellowship.

- They showed commitment and purpose.
- They were hungry to learn.
- The church was important to them.
- They joined in holy communion all together and in their homes.
- They were dedicated in prayer.
- They were full of wonder and reverence.
- They expected, and saw, miracles.
- They were united.
- They sat loose to their possessions, and were generous.
- They met daily for traditional worship in public.
- They ate meals together.
- They were full of joy and constantly praised God.
- The quality of their lives encouraged other people to join them.

I have just gone through that list, giving my own church a mark out of
ten for each aspect. Overall it only scored 39 per cent.

I tried the same test for my own life, smugly expecting to do better.
I scored exactly the same! I need to pray first for myself, asking God to
show me how my spiritual life is draining away and to refill me with
his Spirit. Then I can ask him to show me how to pray for others in my
church, and for renewal in its life and joy.

....

Lord, please refresh my love for   Read 1 Peter 2:4–5, 9, and be
you, and show me how I can   inspired!
enhance the life of the con-   RG
gregation of which I am a part.

Confidence in God

'If we are being called to account today for an act of kindness shown to a cripple and are asked how he was healed, then know this, you and all the people of Israel: It is by the name of Jesus Christ, whom you crucified but whom God raised from the dead, that this man stands before you healed.'

Do you wish you shared the buzz of excitement we read about yesterday? Today's passage is part of another exciting story that I think shows us some of the secrets of that vitality.

The story starts at the beginning of chapter 3, with the dramatic healing of a 40-year-old beggar who had been crippled from birth. Not surprisingly, a crowd gathered as the news spread: the man whom they all knew was running and in the temple area! Peter immediately preached to the crowd about Jesus. Many responded, but Peter and John were arrested, imprisoned overnight and brought before the Jewish leaders next morning. Peter's reply to their questioning is clear, confident and direct. 'Jesus is the source of this miracle!'

So what is the secret of their confidence? Wholeheartedness. Peter was 'filled with the Holy Spirit'. There were no half-measures in his openness to God, or in his belief about Jesus. Read verse 12. Such definiteness about Jesus' uniqueness may not be politically correct, but it is the bedrock of our assurance about our faith. Jesus said of himself, 'No one comes to the Father except through me' (John 14:6). There were no half-measures in Peter's desire to obey God, either. The authorities, caught between the widely known miracle and their desire for this Jesus-faith to be suppressed, lamely told Peter and John to keep quiet. 'We can't! We must obey God!' was their reply. Finally, there were no half-measures in their prayer. There was no long discussion about what they should do. They turned straight to the Sovereign God. Read verses 30 and 31 to see what they asked for and how God answered.

....

Lord, there are often half-measures in my relationship with you, in my faith, in my obedience, in my readiness to pray. Please forgive me, and change me by your Spirit.

RG

Generosity and encouragement

No one claimed private ownership of any possessions, but everything they owned was held in common. With great power the apostles gave their testimony to the resurrection of the Lord Jesus, and great grace was upon them all. There was not a needy person among them.

As you look around the members of your church do you mentally compartmentalize them into the 'spiritual ones' and those who 'do good works'? Do you fit yourself into either of those categories? Christians have different gifts, different temperaments, different opportunities; but it is clear that spiritual power and generous compassion went hand in hand in this church in Jerusalem. Read 6:1–7, where we find the apostles delegating practical care for the widows to men specially chosen for this task—men who were 'full of the Spirit and of wisdom'.

Luke introduces us to a generous man, who is never again referred to by his real name Joseph, but always by his nickname Barnabas, the encourager. Whenever we meet him, he is helping to build the church by his encouragement. In 9:27 we find him affirming the authenticity of Saul's conversion to the suspicious Christians. In 11:22–26 he is sent by the church leaders to assess the situation in Antioch; he stayed to encourage them and he brought Paul to help in the teaching (thereby bringing him into the forefront of leadership). As a missionary with Paul he took his nephew John Mark as a junior assistant. So strongly did he want to encourage Mark after his first failure (13:13), he even parted company with Paul in order to give Mark a second chance (15:37–39).

Do you know anyone you might nickname Barnabas? I can think of one woman in her mid-80s whom I have known for 40 years. Barbara is a 'Barnabas', always bringing encouragement by her generosity and affirmation. I don't think I have ever heard a word of criticism from her. We may not all have that trait naturally, but we can cultivate it as a beautiful flower, while pouring weed-killer on any habit of criticism.

....

If you are the 'spiritual' type, how can you cultivate practical care and encouragement? If you are naturally the 'practical doer', how can you develop in spirituality and wisdom?

RG

A new way of life

[Ananias] said, 'The God of our ancestors has chosen you… You will be his witness to all people of what you have seen and heard. And now what are you waiting for? Get up, be baptized and wash your sins away, calling on his name.'

How would you tell your story to a hostile audience? Paul was in danger of being lynched by a mob in Jerusalem, and the Roman soldiers tried to take him into the safety of the barracks. He wanted to speak first to the crowd. He established his credentials of respectability by speaking to the Roman officer in Greek, then attracted the crowd's attention by using their own language, Aramaic.

The way Paul told his story gives us a framework for our own testimony. He spoke first about what his attitude to God used to be (vv. 2–6). Then he told them how Jesus attracted his attention (vv. 7–10). Next he spoke of the ways other people helped him (vv. 11–16), and finally how God led him forward (vv. 17–21). You might like to think about your own story with this pattern. I remember my conventional churchgoing background; a sermon on Zacchaeus which showed me that I, like him, needed to ask Jesus into my life; the student who was a particular help to me; and many changes since then, including opening more fully to the Holy Spirit, and the spring-cleaning of a cesspool of anger.

Luke thought the story of Saul's conversion important enough to include it three times in Acts. Each Christian's story is different, and each one is valid. Our hearers may not agree with our viewpoint, but they cannot deny our experience. The crowd listened attentively until Paul reached the crunch point of the Lord's commission: 'Go, I will send you to the Gentiles.' That was what many Jews could not stomach. They had been taught that they were God's special people. In their eyes the despised Gentiles had no relationship with God unless they adopted Jewish practices. The thought of reaching out to them was anathema.

....

Think through the main details of your own journey of faith, and thank God for the ways he has met you and changed you.

RG

Power and love in action

[In Lydda Peter] found a man named Aeneas, a paralytic who had been bedridden for eight years. 'Aeneas,' Peter said to him, 'Jesus Christ heals you. Get up and tidy up your mat.' Immediately Aeneas got up. All those who lived in Lydda and Sharon saw him and turned to the Lord.

Have you ever prayed for someone to be miraculously healed? Maybe your prayer was answered in the way you hoped; perhaps you were disappointed. We do not normally understand why the Sovereign God chooses to heal one person but not another, whether miraculously or through medical skill. I am sure that he always hears our prayer, always acts in love and wisdom and never makes a mistake. He certainly still does miracles today. I remember a student with severe head injuries— expected to die, or at best to live with brain damage. Late one afternoon my husband and a friend went into the ward to pray for her as she lay in a coma. Next morning she was eating breakfast; by lunchtime she was sitting in a chair. Her recovery was the talk of the hospital.

It was rather like that with Aeneas and Dorcas. We have seen earlier how the church grew through clear, definite preaching of Jesus' death and resurrection. These verses show us how the gospel spread, too, through the demonstration of God's power to heal. The way Peter acted with both Aeneas and Dorcas reminds us of Jesus with the paralysed man and with Jairus' daughter (Matthew 9:1–8, 23–26). In both cases the news spread and many local inhabitants became believers.

I wish I could have met Dorcas whose story is told in this passage. I picture her as a warm-hearted woman, full of God's love, first busy with needle and thread, then visiting the widows with her gifts. They weren't just crying about 'no more new clothes'. They had lost a friend who cared, who had time for them. Do you make time to visit or phone the lonely and the needy? I often fail.

....

Lord, I pray that I may be open to the ways you want to work through me to help build your Church.

RG

A non-exclusive gospel

Peter began to speak: 'I now realize how true it is that God does not show favouritism but accepts people from every nation who fear him and do what is right'... When they heard this, they had no further objections and praised God, saying, 'So then, God has granted even the Gentiles repentance unto life.'

While it was Paul who was specially called to take the gospel to the Gentiles, the first breakthrough came through Peter—though God had to work hard to make him pay attention! With Paul it was different. God's difficult job with him was to woo him to Christ. Once that happened Paul appeared to find it surprisingly easy, considering his Pharisaic upbringing, to accept his commission to the Gentiles.

It is hard for us to understand just how difficult it was for the Jews to accept the Gentiles. 'Eat with them? Not at all costs!' was their attitude. The nearest parallel I can think of is the reluctance of citizens of occupied countries in World War II to fraternize with the Germans. Peter disputed with God in his vision when he was told to eat animals that were strictly forbidden in the Old Testament. Once he yielded on that, he was ready to accept the remarkable timing of the arrival of Cornelius' messengers and to invite them into his home, to sleep and to eat. When he went with them he found in Caesarea a roomful of the centurion's friends and relations eager to hear about Jesus, open to the Holy Spirit and ready to respond.

It is worth remembering that we read the stories in Acts as insiders, from a Christian viewpoint. But without this breakthrough in their attitude to the Gentiles, we—the non-Jews—would still be the outsiders. Yet despite our centuries of Christian background, we are often less ready than Cornelius and his friends were to respond to Jesus and his Spirit. Galatians 3:26–29 sums up our privileged relationship: *'All* children of God... *all* one in Christ Jesus.'

....

Father, thank you that Jesus is for everyone. Please show me how my own attitude is exclusive towards those who have as much right to be in your family as I have.

RG

First called Christians

Men from Cyprus and Cyrene went to Antioch and began to speak to Greeks also, telling them the good news about the Lord Jesus. The Lord's hand was with them, and a great number of people believed and turned to the Lord.

Last evening we were discussing in our home group the question 'How can we try to change society?' We felt somewhat overwhelmed. What can I, one ordinary individual, do to tackle such a big challenge? Perhaps these early Christians who went to Antioch can give us part of the answer. Some came from Jerusalem, driven out by severe persecution (8:1); they spoke about Jesus only to Jews. Others, travellers from Cyprus and Libya, talked with Gentiles. One-to-one the message spread. The seed of the gospel does not always take root so readily, but 'the Lord's hand was on them' and a new church was soon planted in this thriving cosmopolitan city in Syria (now Antakya, in the southeast tip of Turkey)—a church that was to become the centre of a new missionary movement.

How did this church become so well established? First, Barnabas was sent by the elders in Jerusalem to investigate the situation in Antioch, with Jews and Gentiles worshipping together. Then, seeing the need for a regular instructor for the new converts, he took a 500-km round trip to Tarsus to bring his protégé Saul to share a year's consistent teaching. This church was open to spiritual gifts. Agabus, one of a travelling group of prophets, predicted a widespread famine. The Christians responded with a generous gift for their fellow believers in Judea (although the famine would have included their own area) and sent their two main teachers to take the gift.

Perhaps most important of all, these believers were nicknamed 'Christians'—Christ-people—as they displayed Christ-like character and as they talked about him.

....

Lord, I pray that I may be worthy of the name of Christian: Christ-like in my attitudes, my speech and my behaviour.

Read Acts 8:26–40 to see a detailed example of one-to-one evangelism.

RG

A mission-minded church

While they were worshipping the Lord and fasting, the Holy Spirit said, 'Set apart for me Barnabas and Saul for the work to which I have called them.' So after they had fasted and prayed, they placed their hands on them and sent them off.

Last year the small church in our village had a new experience: a group of twelve men and women went to another congregation for a week to talk about our faith. Most of us were 'ordinary' lay people who had never done anything like it before. We were invited into coffee mornings, lunches, a boat trip, an evening BBQ, a wine bar and many other settings to talk about Jesus and what he meant to us. We trust we helped those who listened. We know we returned enormously strengthened in our own faith and fellowship.

But it was important not only for those who went. The backing of the rest of the congregation was vital. They commissioned us before we left; they prayed for us, together in church and on their own at home; and they were eager to hear the news when we returned.

The leadership team in Antioch came from extraordinarily varied backgrounds: a Levite from Cyprus, a dark-skinned African, an Arab from Libya, a man schooled with royalty, and an ex-Pharisee. But as they fasted (showing they were serious with God) and worshipped (open to God) they heard a clear message from the Spirit: 'Send out your two main teachers for evangelism elsewhere.' They responded immediately, sending off Barnabas and Saul with prayer for the new sphere of service.

First the couple went to Cyprus, then to Turkey. They travelled through southern Turkey, evangelizing initially the Jews and converts to Judaism with mixed success. Eventually they set sail from Attalia (the modern Antalya) to report back to the Christians in Antioch, who were just as eager to hear the news as our own church at home.

....

Lord, please show me how I can not only share your good news myself, but also how I can motivate others to do the same.

                                                                                    RG

41

An important debate

Certain individuals came down from Judea to Antioch and were teaching the believers: 'Unless you are circumcised, according to the customs taught by Moses, you cannot be saved.' This brought Paul and Barnabas into sharp dispute and debate with them.

Have you ever thought you had persuaded a friend to see things your way, when back she comes a week later with the same old arguments in favour of her traditions and prejudices? For these early Christians, the most thorny question was how to accept the Gentiles into the Church. The issue had been raised before, after Peter's visit to Cornelius. Then the traditionalists had appeared to accept Peter's explanation and to welcome the Gentiles (11:1, 2, 18). Now they said, 'No circumcision, no salvation.' In effect, 'Jesus alone is not enough. You must conform to Jewish practices first.'

The debate in Jerusalem was fierce. Perhaps the most relevant thing for us is to see how they settled an argument that might have split the Church apart, as they listened to one another and accepted a wise solution. Four major spokesmen turned the course of the discussion. Peter reminded them of his visit to Cornelius: 'God showed that he accepted them by giving them the Holy Spirit, just as he had to us… It is through the grace of our Lord Jesus Christ that we are saved, just as they are.' Barnabas and Paul told of their experience of God at work in Antioch. And finally James was given deep spiritual wisdom to offer a solution. At first sight, the prohibitions he suggests may look a strange choice, but what do they cover? Avoid any connection with alternative spiritualities; keep sexually pure; show respect for both life and the atonement (Leviticus 17:11). Good basic principles for Christian behaviour.

....

Lord, thank you that the way they settled their argument has affected the way I am accepted in the Church today.

Read Galatians 6:12–15 to see the importance of an inner change rather than the outward mark of circumcision.

RG

Train the next generation

Barnabas wanted to take John, also called Mark, with them, but Paul did not think it wise to take him, because he had deserted them in Pamphylia and had not continued with them in the work... [Paul] came to Derbe and then to Lystra, where a disciple named Timothy lived... Paul wanted to take him along on the journey.

Who nurtured you when you were a new Christian? Who encouraged you into any sphere of ministry? I am forever grateful to Mary, a fellow student who did both for me some decades ago. I was shy and insecure, but enthusiastic to learn. She pushed me straight into praying aloud when I committed my life to Christ, she spent many hours answering my questions, she helped me in Bible reading, and I was only six weeks old in my faith when she asked me to lead the small group Bible study one evening. She gave me a lot of help, and I don't suppose I led it well—but I was launched!

Mary shared Barnabas' and Paul's heart for developing younger Christians. First there was Barnabas' nephew, John Mark. When he let them down, Paul was angry and refused to take him on their second journey, but Barnabas gave him another chance. It paid off, and years later Paul changed his opinion; he wrote to Timothy (by then a leader in the church at Ephesus), 'Get Mark and bring him with you, because he is helpful to me in my ministry' (2 Timothy 4:11).

Paul saw the potential in the young man, Timothy, despite his natural timidity (2 Timothy 1:6–8). As he mentored his 'true son in the faith' (1 Timothy 1:2) he saw him grow in the faith and he was able to entrust him with increasing responsibility in ministry and leadership.

It is vital for the future of our churches that younger people—including small children—are encouraged and helped in this way. Whom could you help to develop in Christian knowledge, experience and service? Are you willing to invest time in them, to take risks with them?

....

Lord, please show me what younger people I can help in their faith and encourage in Christian service.

RG

Hospitality and nurture

[In Corinth, Paul] met a Jew named Aquila, a native of Pontus, who had recently come from Italy with his wife Priscilla… because he was a tentmaker as they were, he stayed and worked with them… [In Ephesus] they invited [Apollos] to their home and explained to him the way of God more adequately.

Aquila and Priscilla were a remarkable couple, whose home was always a place of hospitality. He was a Jew from northern Turkey, taken to Rome as a slave but later freed. She was the daughter of a noble Roman family. They both became Christians, but had to leave Rome after an imperial edict evicting all the Jews from the city. In Corinth they welcomed Paul, who lived and worked with them for 18 months, using their home as a base for evangelizing both Jews and Gentiles.

When Paul left Corinth for Ephesus, Priscilla and Aquila went with him, and there they exercised another ministry in their home. Apollos was a clear speaker and teacher with a good knowledge of the Old Testament, but he had a big gap. He knew nothing about the Holy Spirit. ('He knew only the baptism of John'—and later his disciples told Paul, 'We have not even heard that there is a Holy Spirit' [19:2]). So this hospitable couple invited him to their home. They introduced him to the Holy Spirit, led him into a fresh experience, and then wrote a letter of introduction to their Christian friends in Corinth.

The third setting in which they used their home comes out later in Paul's letters, as he sent greetings to the 'church that meets at their house' in Ephesus and, similarly, to their house-church in Rome. In both cities they opened their home as a meeting place for the Christians.

A home for a guest to stay in; a home for one-to-one discipleship and nurture; a home for a group of Christians to meet. That is the three-fold example they give us. How might you use your home to serve people and to serve God?

....

Lord, please show me how you want me to use my home to build your Church and to further your kingdom.

Read Romans 12:13 and 1 Peter 4:9–10 to underline the message.

RC

A sad farewell

'I have not hesitated to proclaim to you the whole will of God. Keep watch over yourselves and all the flock of which the Holy Spirit has made you overseers. Be shepherds of the church of God which he bought with his own blood.'

It was a solemn occasion. Paul, en route to Jerusalem, did not expect to see the church leaders from Ephesus again. His farewell charge to them looks back over the years he had spent with them and looks forward to their responsibility in continuing to build the church. His final goal for his own life was 'that I may finish the race and complete the task the Lord Jesus has given me'—the commission given to him on the road to Damascus, to tell others about Jesus.

As you read his charge to these leaders you may feel, 'I'm not a leader. This isn't relevant for me.' But whatever our circumstances each one of us is in a position to encourage at least one other person in her faith. Here are some of the things he told them to heed.

- Keep watch over yourselves—in holiness, in guarding the truth.
- Keep watch over the flock—alert to other 'sheep' who might be wandering.
- Don't be afraid to warn those who are in danger.
- Don't be afraid to show your emotions.
- Hold fast to God's word.
- Work hard.
- Be more ready to give than to take.

What would you want to say to people you were about to leave forever, to warn and encourage them? Is there a phrase here you would like to have written on your tombstone? I sometimes think that Paul must have been a difficult person to live and work with. But their tears as they said 'goodbye' show us how much they loved him.

....

Lord, I pray that I may share Paul's dedication, his passion and his willingness to work hard.

RG

The building process

Being church is a dynamic process that shapes us as individuals and the communities in which we live.

'God is building a home. He's using us all—irrespective of how we got here—in what he is building. He used the apostles and prophets for the foundation. Now he's using you, fitting you in brick by brick, stone by stone, with Christ Jesus as the cornerstone that holds all the parts together. We see it taking shape day after day—a holy temple built by God, all of us built into it, a temple in which God is quite at home' (Ephesians 2:19–22, THE MESSAGE).

If you've ever watched a builder at work or built a wall yourself, you'll know that the building process can be a messy business. Sometimes bricks need to be cut to fit, then the mortar takes their uneven shapes and holds them all together to withstand the worst weather.

When we are built together into the living temple—the Church—inhabited by God, the Holy Spirit holds us all together. Although the media sometimes highlight the messy business of the building process, all over the world there are dynamic examples of God's people being built together; united as the body of Christ.

Look at Colossians 3:12–15 for the recipe for perfect unity:

'Clothe yourselves with compassion, kindness, humility, gentleness and patience. Bear with each other and forgive whatever grievances you may have against one another. Forgive as the Lord forgave you. And over all these virtues put on love, which binds them all together in perfect unity. Let the peace of Christ rule in your hearts, since as members of one body you were called to peace. And be thankful.'

In Christ, we have a new individual and corporate identity. We are citizens of a kingdom that cannot be shaken. What is that kingdom like? Over the next fortnight Margaret Killingray will be exploring what it means when we pray: 'Your kingdom come...'

Your kingdom come

'But when you pray, go into your room, close the door and pray to your Father… "Our Father in heaven, hallowed be your name, your kingdom come, your will be done on earth as it is in heaven…"'

I wonder how many times these words have been said and in how many different languages. And yet many of us probably say them so automatically we don't stop to think what they mean.

Over the next two weeks we are going to explore the kingdom of God and especially what it means for the daily lives of Christians, subjects of the King. We will look at different passages in our search. We may discover there are aspects of kingdom life we have never fully understood. Will we have to change how we live as we learn more about God's rule and reign?

Sarah always wanted to be a doctor; she watched the doctors in disaster situations on TV and longed to be able to bring help and healing as they did. As a Christian she prayed very hard that God would help her to achieve her aim. But she found the schoolwork required to get the grades and the years it would take to reach her goal too much and gave up trying, although she still went on praying about it. Of course, Sarah may have needed other advice about the wisest course for her. But many of us, in the same way, pray earnestly for something important, believe God will answer us, and yet do not see there is a part for us to play in bringing it about. I pray, as millions do, in the words of the Lord's Prayer, 'Father I want your kind of world; I want your will to be done everywhere, and I mean it.' But as I pray I have to realize I am committing myself to work with every gift and skill I have to make that prayer come true and bring the kingdom of heaven to earth.

Lord, I long to see your kingdom come and your will done in the lives of those I meet today. Help me to be part of the answer to that prayer.

Read Philippians 2:12–16, where Paul talks about how God works with us to change the world.

MK

Where *is* this kingdom?

Jesus answered, 'My kingdom is not from this world. If my kingdom were from this world, my followers would be fighting to keep me from being handed over to the Jews. But as it is, my kingdom is not from here.'

As Jesus stood before Pilate on trial for his life, the two men had a brief discussion about kingship and kingdoms. Pilate was a powerful ruler, the representative of one of the world's greatest empires. He could do exactly what he liked with Jesus. Roman soldiers awaited his command to flog and to crucify, and would carry it out immediately. Yet he hesitated, unsure how to handle this unusual prisoner. Jesus told Pilate he was indeed a king, who could have called on thousands of angels to rescue him. He may have been the accused, the victim, but he knew exactly what he was doing and why. In fact Pilate had no power over Jesus. Jesus had chosen to go through suffering and death, before he returned to the throne of heaven, making it possible by that death for anyone to enter his kingdom.

Jesus' kingdom was not from this world, but from his Father in heaven. Many of his Jewish followers had been longing for a leader, a Messiah, who would restore the ancient kingdom of Israel and throw out the Romans. Jesus repeatedly had to tell them he wasn't that kind of king. His kingdom was not an earthly state, but is anywhere where God reigns, where his authority is accepted and his will is obeyed. In heaven his kingdom is complete because he is Lord of all. But on earth the kingdom is still not complete, so we pray, 'your kingdom come'.

Jesus is the king of kings, the only true king, the son of the one true God. As he stands before Pilate he is choosing the way of sacrificial love, through suffering and death, so that anyone can enter the kingdom of God through him. His kingdom, God's great plan to redeem all creation, had begun.

....

Lord, I bow in worship and adoration before you, my one true king. I thank you for taking on human life and death, and making a way for me to enter your kingdom.

MK

Kingdom entry qualifications (part 1)

People were bringing little children to him in order that he might touch them; and the disciples spoke sternly to them… Jesus… said to them, 'Let the little children come to me; do not stop them; for it is to such as these that the kingdom of God belongs.'

In this passage, which we look at over two days, people come to Jesus, first little children, who probably don't know what it's all about, are brought to him for blessing; second, a man, eager to enter the kingdom and find eternal life, comes and kneels before Jesus.

In writing his Gospel, Mark introduces us to a number of people who were outcasts of one kind or another—people not accepted in 'proper' social and religious circles, the 'sinners' and the insignificant: tax collectors collaborating with the Romans, prostitutes, lepers who had to live away from home, the handicapped, the demon-possessed, and little children. Jesus healed them, welcomed them, touched them and restored them to family and society. Jesus' arms were open to everyone.

So when the disciples tried to stop people bothering Jesus with children, he was indignant, and not only welcomed them, took them in his arms and blessed them, but said that no one could enter the kingdom unless they were willing to become like a little child. What is it about a small child we have to copy in order to come to Jesus? What particular child-like characteristics did he mean? Dependence? Innocent trust? Lack of self-importance? Vulnerability? Helplessness? Perhaps it is a combination of all these.

Above all, Jesus called people to repent, which means acknowledging dependence and helplessness. We would like to think we could enter the kingdom on merit—as adults with wisdom and experience. No, said Jesus, you have to come with no credentials, no clout and no claims. The more we are sure of our status and our rights, the more difficult it is to enter the kingdom, as we shall see tomorrow.

....

Nothing in my hand I bring, Simply to your cross I cling;
Naked come to you for dress; Helpless, look to you for grace.
Foul, I to the fountain fly; Wash me, saviour, or I die.
Augustus M. Toplady (1740–78)

MK

Kingdom entry qualifications (part 2)

Jesus, looking at him, loved him and said, '… go, sell what you own, and give the money to the poor, and you will have treasure in heaven; then come, follow me.' When he heard this, he was shocked and went away grieving, for he had many possessions.

The church-based toddlers' group attracted a wide range of carers. Some of the mothers were career professionals, well into their 30s, with their first child. They had beautiful houses and cars, and plenty of money. One morning there was an introduction to church activities and afterwards a young new mother said, 'I can't go to church because I'm not married.' She thought she wasn't wanted because she had failed to be 'good'. The professional women *expected* to be welcomed.

In Mark's story an attractive wealthy, young (according to Matthew), influential (according to Luke) man came to Jesus. He honoured Jesus, called him teacher and knelt before him. He appeared sincere—not trying to catch Jesus out as some did—and asked what he could do to enter the kingdom of God, to inherit eternal life. He lived a moral life, obeying God's laws. But the answer was not praise for his achievements, nor an automatic welcome for this attractive and successful person. Jesus asked him to do the one thing he simply could not bear to do—give away his wealth, his security, and his investment in the future and give to the poor.

We cannot enter the kingdom if we put other things before Jesus. We cannot come if we are sure we are good. We can only come if we are willing to lay our entire lives at his feet, acknowledging we are failures. There may be things that matter too much and stop us responding to Jesus' call. It can be money, career, security, a fast lifestyle, but it can even be home, parents and nation. So the young mother in the toddler group, who in humility sensed her own inadequacy, was closer to the kingdom than the attractive young man who loved being wealthy.

....

Pray that those who think they are good enough to enter the kingdom find true childlikeness, and the strength to give up anything that matters too much.

Read Matthew 13:1–23 to see Jesus' explanation of the different ways people respond to the message of the kingdom.

MK

Pictures of the kingdom

He told them another parable: 'The kingdom of heaven is like yeast that a woman took and mixed in with three measures of flour until all of it was leavened.'

Have you listened to someone teaching something important, like how to manage a computer program, using different explanations and word pictures? This is how Jesus taught about the kingdom of God.

The kingdom is like a man sowing his field; like a mustard seed; like yeast in the bread dough; like buried treasure; like a merchant looking for pearls; like a net catching all kinds of fish. Jesus is saying that these pictures will help us understand what it is like when God is at work building his kingdom.

We can sometimes feel our churches are very small and have little impact on the world. I expect some of Jesus' disciples wondered how they could possibly spread this message throughout the whole world when they were so few and so ordinary. Yes, said Jesus, it is very small, but the kingdom is the power of God and it will grow. Like a woman making bread for 100 people with a small lump of yeast; like a tiny mustard seed that grows into a bush big enough for the birds. Acts and words of love, faithful prayer by one not very important person can, with the Holy Spirit's power, change the world.

Life is rather humdrum, prayer seems routine and dry, what difference does it make that I am a Christian? Listen, said Jesus, being part of God's family, part of the kingdom, is just like finding hidden treasure buried in a field. Thrilled, amazed and over the moon, you would hastily buy the field and dig this wonderful treasure up. Or it is like a pearl collector, who against all the odds finds the most wonderful pearl he has ever seen, so he sells everything he has in order to buy it.

Fill me with joy and delight, Lord, because I have found the greatest treasure—knowing you.

Read Acts 2 and see how the mustard seed began to grow and the yeast began to work in the dough.

MK

51

Waiting for the kingdom to come

'See, the home of God is among mortals. He will dwell with them as their God; they will be his peoples, and God himself will be with them; he will wipe every tear from their eyes.'

'The kingdom of this world is to become the kingdom of our Lord and of his Christ, and he shall reign for ever and ever. King of kings and Lord of lords'—words from Revelation sung in the Hallelujah Chorus from Handel's *Messiah*. Revelation rings with the mighty triumph of the Lord, when all will see Jesus as King and bow before him. One day there will be a new heaven and a new earth; his kingdom will have come and all his disciples, subjects of the King, will see his triumph and praise him forever. Jesus spoke about that day when he would come back, when history would end, evil would be judged, but he warned that we will not know when that time will be.

Jesus said, 'It is like a man going on a journey, when he leaves his home and puts his slaves in charge, each with his work, and commands the doorkeeper to be on the watch. Therefore, keep awake—for you do not know when the master of the house will come.'

I well remember going on holiday by car; several hours from journey's end, little voices from the back, would start saying 'Are we nearly there?' at frequent intervals. Life's journey can feel long and tedious, especially when we know there is a wonderful welcome party waiting for us in the promised kingdom. There are many Christians who face hard situations, when the kingdom seems far away. The problems of daily living and everyday relationships can make us feel depressed enough to wonder whether God is still at work bringing in his kingdom. When those days come, we need to renew our vision. Look again at Jesus before Pilate and remember the resurrection; look again at the promises of the final triumph of the kingdom, and sing the Hallelujah Chorus!

....

When being a Christian is hard work, Lord, help me to remember that I already live your resurrection life and that one day we will all sit down at your banquet when the kingdom has come.

MK

The church and the kingdom

As God's chosen ones, holy and beloved, clothe yourselves with com-passion, kindness, humility, meekness and patience. Bear with one another and, if anyone has a complaint against another, forgive each other; just as the Lord has forgiven you, so you also must forgive. Above all, clothe yourselves with love…

There is a problem for us in the English translations of the letters of Paul, James, Peter and John. Most of *our* letters—and phone calls and e-mails—are talking personally to us as individuals. So we are used to hearing the word 'you' and thinking it means 'me'. But the 'you' of these letters is not singular but plural—they are speaking to 'us'—to the fellowship of Christians in local churches.

Be devoted to one another; live in harmony with one another; carry each other's burdens; forgive one another; admonish one another, says Paul. Don't slander one another; pray for each other, says James. Love each other deeply; offer hospitality to one another, says Peter. Love one another, they all say over and over again. They are not talking about the neighbourhood, nor even the family, but the Church.

Together we are being shaped into a living picture of kingdom life, where the character of the King can be seen in the lives of the people of God. The church is where the kingdom begins, where the Holy Spirit works in the lives, not just of individuals, but of the group. From the church we go out to show the world what God's justice, mercy, love and forgiveness mean in every part of life. The church fellowship is where, in praise and worship, we renew and revive our vision of the Lord, ruling the world, sovereign over all, King of kings.

So the work of the kingdom begins in the local fellowship of believ-ers, a place where we can, in our commitment to one another, learn how to be kingdom workers, so that we can go out and live kingdom lives at home, at school, at work and in every corner of the world.

....

Lord, build your church, so that we, with strong and loving roots there, can build your kingdom.

Read 1 Peter 2:4–10, a description of living stones being built into a spiritual house.

MK

Called to build the kingdom

'You are the light of the world. A city built on a hill cannot be hid. No one after lighting a lamp puts it under the bushel basket, but on the lampstand, and it gives light to all in the house.'

The conversation in the supermarket canteen got around to what everyone would be doing at the weekend. Two friends, members of a local church, caught each other's eye. They knew what some of the younger members of the staff did, and knew the response of disbelief and embarrassment if they mentioned the youth group they ran or that the church shared lunch on Sunday.

How could they be salt and light for the kingdom when most of their colleagues despised Christians as weak hypocrites and the Church as judgmental and intolerant? Once when one of them had invited a lonely young man to come to a church barbecue, someone had jumped to protect him, as if they were leading him into a secret sect.

In their home group they started a discussion on how they could reach people who had such strong opinions. As they talked and prayed they realized they had to start by simply being good friends. It would be a longer and much more sacrificial process than just asking people to come to church events. It would mean spending time and emotional capital, showing that they enjoyed their colleagues' company.

So they worked out a plan; they would accept the general invitation to join the others on a Saturday night, maybe showing they could enjoy themselves without drinking too much. They might ask one or two of their younger colleagues for their advice about some of the problems facing the young people in their youth group. They would be willing to talk about some of their own personal struggles.

They asked the group to pray regularly with them, and the next Monday set out for work with a deep sense of anticipation and excitement. They were kingdom workers and the Lord was with them.

....

Where are you called to be salt and light? Pray for guidance about the best way to share the love of Christ in those places.

MK

Kingdom living—when life is hard

Slaves, accept the authority of your masters with all deference, not only those who are kind and gentle, but also those who are harsh... if you endure when you do right and suffer for it, you have God's approval.

There are situations for some of us that we cannot escape however much we may long to, because all our ways out are blocked. There are people in refugee camps or prison who cannot go home. In some countries there are women married to abusive husbands who cannot divorce or run away. There are people working in bad conditions who cannot afford to lose their jobs. And when we enter the kingdom of God, things don't necessarily change. This was certainly true for the Christian slaves to whom Peter was writing. Peter tells them to follow Jesus' example of patient endurance, even when brutal treatment is unjust.

For most of us our situations may not be as dire as that. But ill health, poverty or being a long-term carer, for example, can wear us down. Submit yourselves to situations you cannot avoid or change, says Peter, and begin to allow the Holy Spirit to give you a sense of deep fellowship with Jesus, because you are sharing his sufferings. This is kingdom living—allowing even the most difficult of circumstances to change us into the likeness of Christ; allowing the Holy Spirit to work in us so that we grow the Spirit's fruit, especially long-suffering, patience and self-control.

But joining the kingdom means we now have brothers and sisters in Christ to pray for us and support us in the hard times. Paul told Christian masters to care for their slaves as fellow subjects of the King, and to free them wherever possible. In today's society we should not accept an abusive boss or a violent husband without seeking practical help. Nor should we ever stand by while others are forced to submit to brutality or bullying, without taking some action ourselves.

....

Help me, Lord, to know when to accept a situation and when to seek to change it, and to know that in doing your will I am living your kingdom life.

MK

Kingdom living—doing good

Conduct yourselves honourably among the Gentiles, so that, though they malign you as evildoers, they may see your honourable deeds and glorify God when he comes to judge.

Some time ago I was waiting at a bus stop in London—no one was queuing and there was a restless crowd pushing forward to get on the bus. I held back to let a rather unsteady elderly woman get on. It was not a popular move—someone dodged round me and jumped on ahead of her and everyone seemed to be irritated.

How do we live good lives publicly? Do we do enough kingdom good deeds for others to notice? Peter is right—sometimes doing good can irritate other people. 'You've given me too much change' may well not be popular in a queue at McDonald's. Some things may never be noticed, but we still need to watch our public behaviour—in our workplaces, schools, and of course in our neighbourhoods. Controlling noise from TVs and radios, considerate car parking, feeding next-door's cat, can do more to spread the kingdom of God than any amount of speaking out.

There is so much we can do to build the kingdom in our communities that isn't difficult—just smiling and greeting people, saying please and thank you, standing back for others, letting other drivers out into traffic, picking up the litter in our street, welcoming newcomers. When we do speak of our faith, if we have failed to be active in doing good, then our words may not mean much to our neighbours.

Kingdom living means living well in a sometimes hostile world. We may be misinterpreted, called 'do-gooders', but we do not know how the Holy Spirit will work his purposes in other people's lives through our faithfulness. When God comes to judge and we all stand before the throne of the kingdom, how many will look back and praise God for something we did?

....

Help me, Lord, to have my eyes and ears open today for ways in which I can demonstrate your kingdom's law of love.

MK

Kingdom living—relationships

Husbands, love your wives, just as Christ loved the church... And fathers, do not provoke your children to anger, but bring them up in the discipline and instruction of the Lord.

The new kingdom life should affect every part of our lives. But sometimes the most difficult place to be kingdom people is within our closest relationships. This passage looks at husbands and wives, parents and children, slaves and masters, showing how close relationships can be transformed by kingdom principles.

In Paul's day the head of the household would usually be the senior man. The household might be involved in growing food, educating children, weaving clothes and making furniture. The father was the boss and his wife, children and slaves were not in a position to challenge him, unless he chose to let them. Wives were subject to their husbands; children and slaves obeyed. They had no choice, and the legal authority to compel lay with the father/husband/master.

I am sure there were a lot of contented households, but having almost absolute power undermines good relationships. Paul emphasized that when people became Christians there had to be change, and the biggest change of all had to come in the attitude of the household head. Yes, he tells wives to be subject to their husbands, children to obey their parents, slaves to obey their masters. But he spends a lot more time telling husbands to love their wives sacrificially and to nourish and tenderly care for them. Fathers are to bring up their children in Christian ways. Masters must remember that both master and slave are equally children of God.

Whatever shape our family is, we are to love those close to us so that they grow and flourish. We should not ride roughshod over them, use them when we need them, override their opinions and insist on our preferences. Love is sacrificial and unselfish: it's a big challenge.

....

Kingdom patterns of loving can radically change our relationships. If there are tensions and bitterness, ask the Lord to use you to change things.

Read Ruth chapter 1 to see how Ruth changed her mother-in-law's life.

MK

Kingdom living—caring for the world

God blessed them, and God said to them, 'Be fruitful and multiply, and fill the earth and subdue it; and have dominion over... every living thing that moves upon the earth... God saw everything that he had made, and indeed, it was very good.

Here is the creation of a wonderful world, where humans, made in the image of God, were to act as stewards to care for and nurture the world they lived in. But it all went wrong and God's great plan of salvation was set in motion. Jesus, who is himself God the creator, one with the Father and the Holy Spirit, came to live a human life, died and rose again to restore the kingdom and release all creation from the bondage of sin.

Human beings, the pinnacle of God's creation, still run the world. But the Fall means that good and bad are mixed up in everything. We can build high-tech hospitals and weapons of mass destruction. We can make jewellery with gold and diamonds, but ruin the landscape as we dig them out. We travel vast distances at speed, but pollute and bring devastating climate change. From the first farmer and carpenter to the astrophysicist and computer programmer, we use all the intelligence and imagination God gave us to understand and delight in our universe —and to spoil it.

Those who belong to the kingdom are called to begin his work of restoration, by caring for his good creation. Of course, many who are not Christians are working to restore the damaged systems and to put right past mistakes as well. To do this, we need to know what is happening. We need to be aware of political and economic issues and to understand environmental issues of pollution and global warming. At a practical level we need to be active in local community projects, to vote in elections, to shop thoughtfully, to use our cars less, to recycle, to support aid agencies. People who care will notice if Christians don't.

....

Help me to rejoice in creativity and care for creation, Lord—as I walk in the countryside, read books, sing and dance, play football and make quilts. You call us to enjoy this wonderful world in so many different ways.

MK

Kingdom living—a life of prayer

The prayer of the righteous is powerful and effective. Elijah was a human being like us, and he prayed fervently that it might not rain, and for three years and six months it did not rain on the earth.

Prayer seems to be a universal human instinct, especially in response to overwhelming situations. But many of us find it difficult to understand what exactly prayer is. Is it us talking to God? Should we be listening to God? If so, how? Do his words come just from the Bible, or does he speak to us through our own minds and feelings? If so, can we trust ourselves to know when we are hearing his voice?

Prayer covers so much and there are many examples in the Bible of different types of prayer—the emotional intensity of adoration and worship, the longings and outpourings of love and gratitude, the cries of despair voiced in the psalms, the grief of repentance. And often, simply people and situations we long for God to change. Remember how Jesus cried out for Jerusalem and its people to turn to him, knowing they wouldn't—not then—and knowing the Romans would destroy the city.

'The prayer of the righteous is powerful and effective,' says James. Forgiven people, kingdom people, are called to pray—and their prayers will work. James describes how Elijah prayed and it stopped raining. He sees Elijah not just as God's prophet, speaking God's words about the drought, but as the instrument by which the drought happened. In another Old Testament example, Abraham bargained with God in prayer over the destruction of Sodom and Gomorrah, and God said he would take notice of what Abraham had prayed and even change his purposes.

So we are called, as builders of the kingdom, to be effective co-workers with God by praying, because amazingly he chooses to use our prayers to make his kingdom come. We really can make things happen, if we accept the call to be informed, self-controlled, powerful and effective pray-ers.

....

You may like to take a Bible prayer (Colossians 1:9–14 or Psalm 121, for example) and turn the words into prayers for friends and family.

MK

Kingdom living—celebrations

Be sure to set aside a tenth of all that your fields produce each year. Eat the tithe... in the presence of the Lord your God... and rejoice. At the end of every three years, bring all the tithes... so that... the aliens, the fatherless and the widows... may come and eat and be satisfied.

I had always thought tithing was about giving a tenth of one's income to Christian causes. When I first read this passage in Deuteronomy I was surprised and delighted to find tithing was also about having a feast with neighbours in the presence of the Lord *and* giving generously to those in need. But this wonderful way to celebrate harvest seems to have been forgotten and eventually tithing became a heavy burden of duty and legalism, so that Jesus warned the Pharisees about giving God a tenth of their mint and rue, but neglecting justice and the love of God.

Christians too can turn kingdom living into a burden of duty, lists of things that cannot be done on a Sunday, formal services using dead liturgy. To put aside an offering for the Lord, and then eat it at a party with friends seems like a recipe for guilt. But, says the Lord, be generous out of joy and pleasure, not out of grudging obedience.

The kingdom of heaven is like a king who prepared a wedding banquet, a picture echoed in Revelation where a great multitude shout, 'Hallelujah! Let us rejoice and be glad! For the wedding of the Lamb has come, and his bride has made herself ready. Blessed are those who are invited to the wedding supper of the Lamb!'

So the kingdom of God is about warm hospitality, about parties with friends, about bringing people who are outside into circles of easy companionship, about inclusive banquets that break down barriers of class, status and race, about a kingdom that people long to join, about a wedding where we, the church, are the bride and Jesus, our Lord and Saviour, is also our bridegroom. What a kingdom!

....

Show me, Lord, how to act with gratitude and generosity as a heartfelt response for all you have given me.

Read Leviticus 19:9 and 10, for another surprising command to be generous.

MK

In partnership

Weddings are a regular feature of the New Testament: Jesus' first miracle was at a wedding and he described 'The kingdom of heaven... like a king who prepared a wedding banquet for his son (Matthew 22:2). As the bride of Christ, the Church is being prepared for a heavenly wedding feast. The invitations have gone out and Jesus longs for a positive response. And he has already gone ahead to prepare a place for us.

To let the full impact of those words sink in, I imagine being a guest at a wedding where I am not sure of who I'll know. I arrive to find the room packed and people partying. I hope I can find a seat to squeeze in somewhere unnoticed. But before I'm even over the threshold, the host is striding towards me, beaming. 'Welcome. Let me show you to the place at the table I've prepared for you. I've been so looking forward to seeing you.'

I tend to think of Jesus preparing a place just for me—though that's my Western individualism showing again. In fact, all believers will be part of Christ's bride; when the Bible says we will be like Jesus, part of our likeness must reflect the fact that Jesus, his Father and the Holy Spirit are always one. He is always in partnership.

In the next two weeks Celia Bowring will be helping us to think about the power of partnership. Celia coordinates a network linking women who are married to church leaders—hence her ability to give some special insights into the impact and strength of partnership.

For some, partnership is a particularly thorny issue: the relationships they have are painful, or they are not in the partnership that they long for. As Celia shows, the Bible gives many different examples of partnerships which work well—and those which are disastrous.

One of the keys to successful partnership—especially the deepest relationships—is that they reflect the Trinity's self-giving love and unity: Jesus concentrates on bringing glory to the Father; the Father's focus is glorifying the Son and the Holy Spirit is busy making Jesus known. Likewise, Jesus wants us to experience that intimacy—hence his challenge: 'As I have loved you, so you must love one another. By this everyone will know that you are my disciples, if you love one another' (John 13:34–35).

Partners with God

So God created human beings in his own image, in the image of God he created him; male and female he created them.

In the following days we will be looking at partnerships found in the Bible. There are married couples, family members, friends and colleagues. Some get on together and some hate each other.

As we start in Genesis, imagine what life would be like if we were created sexless. For a start, a different and probably far less interesting method of reproduction might be necessary. And without the fascinating differences of masculine and feminine, history's civilizations and cultures would have been sadly dull and monochrome. God made us in his own image: Father, Son and Holy Spirit expressed in man and woman together. Adam and Eve were perfectly created for each other, equal but different, Eve the 'helper'—not some inferior assistant but one who enables and empowers. The same word is used in Psalm 115:11: 'The Lord is my helper'.

The human race could have achieved so much in partnership with God, if only Adam and Eve had said 'no' to the forbidden fruit and chosen to obey God. Instead, humanity tragically fell into sin, became separated from God and doomed to die. Men and women were also driven apart—'Your desire will be for your husband, and he will rule over you'—making even the most loving relationships vulnerable to this day.

Jesus, however, treated women with respect and love, knowing how it had been in the beginning and longing to set us free. Male and female are equal at the cross; together reflecting something of God's image once again, with complementary roles and submitting to each other. In Christ's kingdom there is freedom and fulfilment for both men and women, although the Church has not always reflected this truth. Where we work together in partnership, according to our strengths and gifting—human and spiritual—God's kingdom advances.

....

Thank God we are all one in Christ Jesus.

Read Galatians 3:26–29 to see the radical equality we have with each other in Christ.

CB

Sibling rivalry

But the two children struggled with each other in her womb. So she went to ask the Lord about it. 'Why is this happening to me?'

Rebekah was married for 20 years before this pregnancy. She and Isaac longed for a child to fulfil God's promise to his father Abraham that he would have numerous descendents. Being childless was hard in that culture—indeed it can be painful for any woman. Now at last her prayers were answered; Rebekah was carrying twins. I wonder how she dreamed it would be—rosy-cheeked cherubs playing around her, full of laughter and joy... The turmoil within her womb indicated that this wasn't to be. Her sons were at war with each other even then.

Jacob and Esau were central to God's plan. Yet one was a conniving schemer who robbed his brother of his birthright and father's blessing, while the other seemed more interested in chasing deer than following his destiny. Rebekah agonized over her boys and tried to steer events to the advantage of her favourite, Jacob. Isaac preferred Esau. It can't have been a happy family.

Years went by. Rebekah lost her son when he fled to escape the wrath of Esau and she probably missed out on seeing her grandchildren. The account of Jacob's final return and reconciliation with his brother makes no mention of her. Presumably she'd died by then.

Being a godly parent demands great patience, prayerfulness and love. We know our children are not possessions but individuals entrusted to us for a certain time. Perhaps today you are concerned about the lives and relationships of young people close to you—your own or someone else's children. Tempting though it may be to try and control, let's give them back to God to deal with them, according to his purposes.

....

Lord, help me to hold lightly those whom I love. I bring them to you and pray for your will to be done in their lives. Please give me wisdom to understand how to support them as you want me to.

CB

Leaders of Israel

But Moses said to the Lord, 'Since I speak with faltering lips, why would Pharaoh listen to me?' Then the Lord said to Moses, 'See, I have made you like God to Pharaoh, and your brother Aaron will be your prophet.'

Have you heard about the man called by God to serve in some farflung and dangerous country? 'Here am I, Lord!' he responded, 'Send somebody else!' Moses led a good life in Midian; a family man with a secure job as his father-in-law's shepherd, far removed from his extraordinary childhood in Egypt as the adopted son of Pharaoh's daughter. Those memories, the painful awareness of his own people's oppression, and the guilt he carried for the murder he'd committed in a clumsy attempt to help the Hebrew slaves must still have haunted him, though.

When he noticed the flaming bush did he have any inkling that God was about to invade his peaceful existence and thrust him into the midst of one of the most dramatic events of history? Maybe, deep inside, Moses knew this was his destiny. God spoke to him, outlining Moses' key role in the plan for the exodus, and the reality hit him. 'The Hebrews won't accept me as a leader,' Moses protested and, because he refused to go it alone, trusting God to equip him, his brother was allowed to come alongside as his 'prophet'.

Although Aaron was a co-leader of Israel, he had weaknesses. Once the Red Sea was miraculously crossed it was sister Miriam who led the thanksgiving celebration with Moses, not Aaron, even though he became the first priest. While Moses was on Mount Sinai receiving the ten commandments, Aaron supervised the construction of a golden calf idol and encouraged the people to worship it!

Perhaps Moses lived to regret the appointment of Aaron, wishing he had listened to God's original commission to him alone.

....

Lord, if you want me to take the lead in something, please help me to trust you completely and know who to ask to share the responsibility.

CB

Seduced and deceived

Then Delilah pouted, 'How can you say you love me when you don't confide in me? You've made fun of me three times now, and you still haven't told me what makes you so strong!' So day after day she nagged him until he couldn't stand it any longer. Finally, Samson told her his secret.

It is a while since I read this story, and the enormity of both Delilah's treachery and Samson's sheer stupidity hit me afresh. This parody of love, laced with lies and bribery, is a tragic metaphor of how Satan can ensnare those who stray from the protection of God's mercy and grace. The producers of *EastEnders* would be hard pushed to come up with a plot as shocking as this.

Delilah is paid by the Philistine authorities to seduce the man who has caused them so much trouble and discover the secret of his God-given strength. Three times she betrays Samson but he keeps coming back to her, eventually telling her his long hair is the sign of his belonging to God and the source of his power. What kind of spell does Delilah cast on Samson to persuade him to lay his sleepy head on her lap while she organizes a barber to come and shave off his locks? She shows no sorrow and greedily accepts her blood money. The now enfeebled Samson has his eyes gouged out and the Philistines triumphantly drag him away to slave-labour, chained like an animal, in the mills of Gaza. It is a long time before he has the chance to serve God again.

Samson made many mistakes, but falling in love with Delilah was probably his most spectacular. He was so sure of his unassailable strength, he stopped trusting and obeying God. Love—or was it lust?—made him blind long before the Philistines had him at their mercy.

It is so important to form a partnership with the right person in whatever we do, someone with the same values, the same allegiances, the same Lord.

....

Father, save me from the blindness that pride and prejudice can produce.

CB

Loyalty and kindness

But Ruth said, 'Don't force me to leave you; don't make me go home. Where you go, I go; and where you live I'll live. Your people are my people, your God is my god; where you die, I'll die, and that's where I'll be buried.'

What motivated Ruth to stick with Naomi in the way she did? The story of the girl from Moab who became the ancestor of both King David and Jesus Christ has almost a fairytale quality. Ruth was single-minded in her decision to care for her mother-in-law but she was also searching for God. She was willing to turn her back on everything in her past to be identified with Naomi's people, become part of her community in Bethlehem and serve the God of Israel. It was as if the Holy Spirit responded to her loyalty, and although her courage and her commitment were severely tested Ruth ended up as the honoured wife of her protector and redeemer, Boaz.

The story of Ruth is a parable of how Christ rescues us, lovingly watches over us and saves us. She was one of a handful of foreigners to be found in the genealogy of Jesus—a reminder that salvation is available to everyone who seeks him—not just the people of Israel.

Ruth was rewarded for her kindness to Naomi—who always seems to me to be quite a difficult person, at least in the middle part of the story. Changing your name from 'Pleasant' (the meaning of Naomi) to 'Bitter' (Mara) is hardly the attitude of a cheery optimist! The end of the book of Ruth sees Grandma Naomi happily nursing baby Obed for her daughter-in-law who, according to all the neighbours 'is more to you more than seven sons'—praise indeed!

....

Father, may I demonstrate loyalty and kindness in my relationships. Let me be like Jesus, with the help of your Spirit.

Meditate on Proverbs 3:3–7, which reflects the kind of attitude Ruth had.

CB

Comrades in arms

'I grieve for you, Jonathan my brother; you were very dear to me. Your love for me was wonderful, more wonderful than that of women.'

In a few days we will commemorate the Armistice on Remembrance Sunday. The Queen, senior politicians, religious leaders, military chiefs, representatives from Commonwealth countries and members of the public will stand silently before the Cenotaph to remember those who fought and fell in two World Wars and many conflicts since. Simultaneously, around war memorials in villages and towns, in cemeteries, churches and cathedrals, here and overseas, people will ponder and pray about the sacrifices millions made, for freedom and peace.

I shall think of my Dad. He survived the Second World War, but fighting in it scarred him both physically and emotionally. He rarely spoke of it, but when he did the stories were usually about the extraordinary comradeship among soldiers in times of danger and the bravery of many who risked their lives for one another.

A favourite text for this remembrance ceremony is Jesus' words: 'Greater love has no man than to lay down his life for his friends' (John 15:13). He was particularly referring to his own struggle against evil and the sacrifice for sin that he made to give us eternal life—a far more significant act than any battlefield heroism throughout history.

David and Jonathan were warriors; courageous, strong and skilled in the business of subduing enemies and leading others. But beneath the toughness they, like many fighting men, had soft hearts. Their thoughts were for family, for the things that really mattered—like faithful friendship and the cause for which they strove. Jonathan said to David, 'And may you treat me with the faithful love of the Lord as long as I live. But if I die, treat my family with this faithful love' (1 Samuel 20:14, NLT).

....

Father, please watch over those on active service at this time. Bless them, and may you become their greatest friend, especially in the face of danger and fear.

CB

Passing on the baton

Elijah said to Elisha, 'Tell me, what can I do for you before I am taken from you?' 'Let me inherit a double portion of your spirit,' Elisha replied.

The godly influence of some exceptional people spans centuries. Elijah was one such; Jesus likened him to John the Baptist. That won't apply to us all, but God does call all Christians to serve the people of their own time. Pundits nowadays give each generation its own intriguing name—some of them tricky for an old-fashioned 'Baby Boomer' like me to understand. People born in the 1970s are 'Generation X-ers'; and our own children, dating from the '80s, apparently belong to 'Generation Y'. Today's youngsters worship, pray, evangelize and live very differently from how I thought and acted at that age, but life has moved on with breathtaking pace. As today's church (rather than tomorrow's), they need our support to follow Jesus faithfully and wisely in this wild and wacky world. How can we give it effectively?

Elijah prophesied for 55 years, living under the malevolent reign of Ahab and Jezebel, fighting for truth and challenging the worship of Baal. At times he suffered deep depression and isolation, so towards the end of his life God sent Elisha as a companion, and later Elijah's successor. Elisha treated his teacher with immense respect, serving him humbly. The old man's standards were high; he tested Elisha many times and mentored him well, sharing all he had and preparing him to take over once he himself left Planet Earth in that spectacular angelic chariot. Elisha had a remarkable ministry. Thirty-one times, the Bible calls him 'a man of God'—more than anyone else—and he performed twice the miracles Elijah had. He inherited a double portion of Elijah's spirit and you see the similarity in their walk with God. Both were extraordinary—but the younger man followed a different path in a different generation.

....

Father, show me where I can bridge the generation gap and support someone outside my own age group.

Read Mark 9:2–8 to meet Elijah once more.

CB

Unconditional love

I will make you my wife forever, showing you righteousness and justice, unfailing love and compassion. I will be faithful to you and make you mine, and you will finally know me as Lord.

In the seventh century BC, Israel was in a bad way. King Jeroboam II, like his father before and his son after him, 'did what was evil in God's sight'. Elisha was dead but God had raised up four new prophets: Isaiah, Micah, Amos and Hosea. The ministry of Hosea was perhaps the hardest—his own marriage became a parable of how God loved his people, even though they spurned him so carelessly, disregarding his laws and destroying their holy inheritance.

Hosea married a prostitute called Gomer. They had one son, and then two more children: 'Not-loved' and 'Not-my-people'. It is doubtful whether Hosea was the father of any of them.

Imagine Hosea's pain. Here was a God-fearing man, a keeper of the law and a preacher of the truth, betrayed by his wife and shamed in his community. Can you imagine how people talked? Gomer represents Israel, and in chapter 2 God's anger at the faithlessness of his people is expressed by Hosea with deep anguish and longing that she would return to a place of repentance and forgiveness. 'I will win her back once again… lead her out into the desert and speak tenderly to her there. I will return her vineyards to her and transform the Valley of Trouble into a gateway of hope…'

At God's prompting Hosea redeems his runaway wife, whose price is by now very cheap and Gomer is given the opportunity to embrace the one who loves her. We do not know how this domestic drama concludes but perhaps it is as sad as the story of Israel's continuing estrangement from the Husband who keeps on loving anyway; bringing punishment at times and rescue at others. This kind of love is unfathomable—but it is the way God is, never giving up and loving unconditionally.

....

Father, thank you for your   Read Ephesians 3:14–19 to
unconditional love towards me.   remind yourself of the
                                            dimensions of God's love.

                                                                    CB

Preparing the way

'I am the bridegroom's friend, and I am filled with joy at his success. He must become greater and greater, and I must become less and less.'

John was Jesus' cousin. As children they may have been close—perhaps their friendship strengthened Jesus as he gradually grew to recognize who he was and what lay ahead. Maybe they talked about some of these issues and prayed together about the future. We know little about Jesus' first 30 years so this is mere speculation—they may have rarely met. But whoever it was that most influenced young John, he grew into a powerful man of God. People from all over Judea flocked to hear his preaching, confess their sins and be baptized by him. He was fearless, challenging everyone—especially the hypocrites who thought they were better than everyone else. He followed in the footsteps of Israel's great prophets: Isaiah, Jeremiah and the rest.

However, God had special plans for John; to be a kind of holy 'warm-up act' for his cousin, the one 'far greater than I am—so much greater that I am not even worthy to be his slave!' He submitted to God, obedient to the very end. The day Jesus arrived on the river bank to be baptized, John plunged him into the water. Then the Holy Spirit descended like a dove as the Father's voice commended his Son. John the Baptist's cooperation was needed for God to accomplish his will.

John lived for Jesus—and died for his sake too. Jesus had a very high opinion of him: 'I assure you, of all who have lived, none is greater than John the Baptist.' John died ignominiously at the whim of evil Herod Antipas, he was deeply loved by the Lord he served, and mourned by him.

....

God wants to work in partnership with you to bring about his plans. Are you willing?

Read more about John in Isaiah 40:3; Luke 1:5–25; and Mark 6:14–29.

CB

Faithful followers

A woman called Martha welcomed him to her house. She had a sister by the name of Mary who settled down at the Lord's feet and was listening to what he said.

Imagine if Jesus was coming to your house for dinner! It would be only natural to cook your most admired recipes, launder the table linen to a dazzling white, polish the cutlery until it sparkled in the candlelight and extend this fine hospitality to your best friends too.

I empathize with Martha. In her anxiety for everything to be perfect I am sure she managed to spill, overcook and burn crucial dishes on the menu. Then, glancing out of the steaming kitchen she sees her sister relaxing and hanging on Jesus' every word. 'Mary, I need your help!' she complains and I can just hear Jesus insisting that cheese on toast would have been just fine; that he didn't want anyone to be left out of the conversation, especially not to slave away at a hot cooker. He appreciates Martha's loving attention but longs for her to sit with him alongside Mary, and share what is on his heart. Perhaps sometimes we allow busyness to distance ourselves from the Lord.

Later in the Gospels we meet them again. The last thing on Martha's mind now is cooking, for her brother Lazarus is dead. She appeals to Jesus. 'If you had been here he wouldn't have died but even now I know God will give you anything you ask.' She believes he is the Messiah—and always has done. Then her sister Mary, who loves Jesus so much, comes weeping so piteously that Jesus cries too—even though he knows what will happen next—the raising of Lazarus from the dead!

The fact that Jesus came to this ordinary family home is greatly encouraging to me. Mary and Martha were among his most faithful followers and he chose to spend time in their house. May he feel welcome in our homes too.

....

Father, make my home a gateway for others to come into your presence and sit at your feet.

CB

Men of faith

When they saw the courage of Peter and John and realized that they were unschooled, ordinary men, they were astonished and they took note that these men had been with Jesus.

It is good to have a partner. At work, in marriage, to relax with or in undertaking God's work, two are better than one and more than twice as effective. In these two passages we see Peter and John together healing a lame man, getting arrested and locked up, preaching boldly to their opponents and refusing to keep silent about Jesus.

Although Peter is the more vocal, John is also mentioned constantly. We sense the importance of his support and quiet confidence in the partnership. Peter and John witnessed extraordinary miracles and heard amazing teaching. They lived with Jesus and knew him well. John was 'the disciple that Jesus loved'—his close friend—and Peter the one charged to care for the fledgling Church. With James they witnessed Christ's transfiguration. Like the rest they ran away when soldiers came to arrest him, but Peter and John were among the first to find the empty tomb and discover that Jesus had risen from the dead.

We are familiar with Peter's impetuosity, but his story goes from strength to strength throughout Acts and his maturity is further revealed in his two epistles. Peter was full of faith, courageous and big-hearted; and as he became familiar with suffering he learned to consider it joy.

John wrote his Gospel, unique for its insights into God's eternal plan fulfilled through Jesus, and three epistles, all about love. Then we have the book of Revelation, that extraordinary vision of the spiritual realm, full of symbolic visions and praise to the Lamb of God—that very same Lord on whose shoulder he had leaned in Galilee, long years before.

How encouraging that these two humble fishermen, chosen by Jesus himself, were so wonderfully inspired by God, strengthening Christians of all generations since.

....

Pray for those whose partnership you appreciate, asking God to strengthen these relationships, using them to fulfil his plans.

CB

Father and son

Night and day I constantly remember you in my prayers. I long to see you again, for I remember your tears as we parted… Timothy, my dear son, be strong with the special favour God gives you in Christ Jesus.

Paul had many spiritual brothers but one was singled out as his 'son'. Timothy, whose faith had been nurtured by a godly mother and grand-mother, was special to Paul who decided to father him. Paul constantly commits him to God. The power of prayer cannot be exaggerated. Sometimes we may feel a strong urgency to pray for our children in specific ways. The authority of believing parents is considerable and can extend to those who are not physically part of our family but whom God has specially put on our hearts.

Paul commissions Timothy to ministry. Paul refers to an earlier prophecy over Timothy and in these two letters Paul mentions the young man's task to teach and lead about 20 times. Although Timothy is naturally timid, Paul discerns God's calling and encourages him to go confidently forward. 'Teach these great truths to trustworthy people who are able to pass them on to others' (2 Timothy 2:2).

Paul challenges him to holiness. 'Cling tightly to your faith in Christ and always keep your conscience clear' (1 Timothy 1:19). Building on the scriptures he has known since childhood, Timothy must uphold truth and live a pure life, uncompromisingly, with God's help.

Paul confides in him. Paul's loneliness and anxiety in prison come through his words to this beloved son. They are not stern but full of warm affection and expressing his need of encouragement. Paul is honest about his weaknesses and so grateful his spiritual son will always stick by him. 'I have no one else like Timothy who genuinely cares… He has proved himself. Like a son with his father he has helped me in preaching the good news' (Philippians 2:19–22).

....

Has God given you a spiritual parent or child to care for? How can you encourage them today?

CB

73

Marriage and ministry

[Priscilla and Aquila] have been co-workers in my ministry for Christ Jesus. In fact, they risked their lives for me.

We know little about these two Italian Jews but they represent millions of couples down the ages who have served God in partnership together. Both husband and wife were highly regarded by Paul; Priscilla's ministry was as significant as Aquila's although they probably had differing gifts and responsibilities.

Paul was a fellow tentmaker. Arriving in Corinth, he worked with them. As they hemmed tarpaulins and sewed on guy ropes, Paul taught them all they needed to know to become faithful followers of 'The Way'. Aquila and Priscilla then accompanied him to Ephesus, remaining there, using their house as a place for the church to meet, when Paul continued his journey.

One day a preacher called Apollos arrived in Ephesus. He was well-versed in scripture and an enthusiastic evangelist, but the couple realized that he needed a little extra guidance. How easily Aquila and his wife could have deflated this young man; but they spoke to him graciously to correct his teaching and eventually sent him with warm recommendations on to Achaia where he preached powerfully.

But this couple's ministry was not just cosy encouragement; at some point they found themselves in danger because of their commitment to Jesus. Paul acknowledges this in the text at the top of this page.

Few of God's servants are famous; most of us are called to be loving light and effective salt just where we live and work. Christian ministry is not just what we do in church, it is interwoven with everything we do. It's our attitude that counts: selflessness towards others and obedience to God. Like Aquila and Priscilla's help to Paul, our 'tent making' and willingness to serve will be recorded—if not down here, in the ledgers of heaven.

....

Read Ecclesiastes 4:9–12 for further encouragement about the advantages of companionship.

CB

Eternal love

'And I saw the holy city, the new Jerusalem, coming down from God out of heaven like a beautiful bride prepared for her husband.'

[Jesus] gave up his life for her... to present her to himself as a glorious church... holy and without fault.

Today is the last in this series on partnership. From Adam and Eve onwards we have seen the power of relationships, for good or ill. Many of our couples demonstrate wonderful loyalty and compatibility, while others are clearly mismatched, some bringing tragic consequences on the heads of those around them.

Jesus longed for unity among his friends, the kind of loving commitment seen to perfection in the Trinity of Father, Son and Spirit. God's plan, from Eden onwards was always to extend this love to men and women, and here at last, in the final chapters of Revelation, it comes. The bride of Christ, made utterly beautiful and perfect, appears to take her place beside him forever. Every time I watch (usually weeping happily, unashamedly!) a radiant girl walking down the aisle to her fiancé I think of this truth; it's an echo, a promise of what awaits us all in heaven.

You and I are part of this final coming together of Christ and his beloved. Like the Father, Son and Holy Spirit we will love perfectly, united but keeping our individual identity and living life to the full—eternal life it will be—far removed from the darkness of sin. 'The Spirit and the bride say, "Come." Let the thirsty ones come... and drink the water of life without charge' (Revelation 22:17).

There are those who say that goodness is boring. The creative possibilities God has prepared for us in heaven will prove them totally wrong. The wonders of his love will surpass every longing of all the human hearts ever created!

....

Lord Jesus, show me something of how it will be on that day. Give me a glimpse of it. Help me to believe you, hope in you and love you more and more.

CB

Jesus the life giver

In TV programmes like *Big Brother* or *I'm a Celebrity, Get Me Out of Here*, viewers watch the participants vying for the limelight as the virtual community disintegrates. In sharp contrast, God calls us to work together to show the world what he is like. As well as working with each other, we cooperate with the Holy Spirit calling people to come to Jesus— as Revelation 22:17 describes: '"Come!" say the Spirit and the Bride. Whoever hears, echo, "Come!" Is anyone thirsty? Come! All who will, come and drink, Drink freely of the Water of Life!'

Jesus gave the same invitation to people attending the Passover feast in Jerusalem when he stood and said in a loud voice, 'Let anyone who is thirsty come to me and drink. Whoever believes in me, as the scripture has said, will have streams of living water flowing from within' (John 7:37); it was the same promise he gave to the women at the well in Samaria when he said: 'Those who drink the water I give them will never thirst. Indeed, the water I give them will become a spring of water welling up to eternal life' (John 4:14).

It is a wonderful picture: to be like a well that never runs dry; always being refreshed by God as we refresh others. When we encounter Jesus and drink deep from his love, as Isaiah said, 'sharing your food with the hungry, inviting the homeless poor into your homes, putting clothes on the shivering ill-clad, being available to your own families... If you get rid of unfair practices, quit blaming victims, quit gossiping about other people's sins. If you are generous with the hungry and start giving yourselves to the down-and-out, your lives will begin to glow in the darkness.'

Then God promises, 'I'll give you a full life in the emptiest of places— firm muscles, strong bones. You'll be like a well-watered garden, a gurgling spring that never runs dry. You'll use the old rubble of past lives to build anew, rebuild the foundations from out of your past. You'll be known as those who can fix anything, restore old ruins, rebuild and renovate, make the community livable again' (Isaiah 58:7–12, *THE MESSAGE*).

This is what happens when people meet Jesus, as we shall see in the next set of readings.

Meeting people on the street

'We have found the Messiah'... And he brought him to Jesus.

Fishermen. Tax collectors. Soldiers. Prostitutes. Housewives. Rich yuppies. Religious bigwigs. Disabled people. Commuters. The ill and dying. Prison officers. Merchants. When God decided to become incarnate in Jesus Christ, and visit his earth, he was not fussy over whom he met. The Gospels are full of stories of common, corrupt, ordinary people who encountered Jesus—and how meeting him turned their lives upside down.

What I love about the Gospel stories is the very everyday ordinariness of them. Have you ever considered that none of these people had got up that morning and said, 'Today I shall encounter the Messiah, God incarnate. My encounter with him will transform my life, and become known to hundreds of millions of people around the world for centuries to come.' Nothing of the sort. The people whose stories are in the Gospels and Acts were like me, like the people I see in Macclesfield: caught up in the busy, stressed rounds of their daily lives. Some were at work, trying to meet deadlines. Some were considering their investments. Some were ill, in great pain. Others were buying and selling. Still others were even doing shameful things, hoping to keep a low profile. Everyday life; immediate, daily problems.

And yet—and yet, Jesus met them right there in the street. Time and again it was he who approached them. He met them at their point of need, healed them, forgave them, addressed the big issues in their lives, and then called them to 'follow' him. He went to them—so they could come to him.

And they did—by the score. Over the next two weeks let's look at some of the stories in more detail. The stories of people range from disciples to sceptics; from face-to-face encounters with Jesus, to encounters with the risen Christ.

....

What condition were you in when you first encountered Jesus? Where would you be now without him?

Read Hebrews 12:1–12 for a reminder of how other Christians face the problems that you do, and win through.

AC

Do you love me?

As Jesus was walking beside the Sea of Galilee, he saw two brothers, Simon called Peter and his brother Andrew. They were casting a net into the lake, for they were fishermen. 'Come, follow me,' Jesus said.

The night after the dinner party my friend was really upset. She was disgusted with herself. Here she was, a Christian of many years' standing, but when confronted by two highly sophisticated couples who were avowed atheists, she had said nothing.

Excuses didn't work: she'd been tired; she was a guest, so it was better to say nothing. Inside she knew why she'd been silent about her faith: she was simply afraid of their mocking, their inevitable scorn.

Such things happen to many of us: we sincerely love Christ, and alone with him, or with other Christians, we radiate our faith. But plonk us down, alone, in hostile territory, and we are frightened.

Simon Peter knew all about commitment—and fear. When Jesus had chosen him and Andrew first of all the disciples, Simon Peter didn't hang about—he dropped his nets and followed. He was the one who ventured to walk on water, the first disciple to openly declare Jesus was the Messiah, the one who at the transfiguration wanted to commemorate it. No doubt about his love.

But then—the night of the crucifixion, he denied Christ three times. He was alone, on hostile territory, and simply afraid.

Jesus did not condemn him—he just asked him to repeat his commitment: 'Do you love me, Peter?' And then, in Acts, Jesus sent Peter his indwelling Holy Spirit. That changed Peter from a timid disciple to a fearless apostle.

So the solution for us is the same. Simon loved Jesus and wanted to follow him. But it was not until Simon really experienced the power of Christ's indwelling Spirit that he had the power to do so—fearlessly.

....

Jesus called Peter the rock on which he'd build his church. When attempting anything for God's kingdom, let's do it in his strength, not our own.

Read Acts 4:1–21 to discover a Peter whom nobody can silence! He'd make any dinner party a lively event.

AC

Give them the benefit of the doubt

Jesus said, 'It is not the healthy who need a doctor, but the sick…
I have not come to call the righteous, but sinners.'

This year I holidayed in Greece, where I love browsing in the tourist
shops. One was a pottery, run by an English woman. I commented on
what a great life she must have there.

She burst into tears. 'It would be,' she sobbed, 'except for my land-
lady. She is doubling the rent and I don't know how I'll pay. No matter what I sell, she wants most of my profits. I've been here 20 years,
and I've nowhere else to go. I am trapped.'

Power and greed is a frightening combination. If you've ever been
the target of someone with power over your life, and who wants your
money, you'll know what I mean. It's what makes many landlord–
tenant relationships and so many divorces such a nightmare.

No wonder Matthew Levi was not a popular man. He was a Jew
who worked as a tax collector for the Roman empire—a job which in
those days was corrupt. His greed for money had led to him turning on
his own kind, oppressing his own people. The Jews viewed him with
fear and disgust, but Jesus went straight over to him, and said 'Follow
me'. You'd think Levi would have told Jesus to get lost. Yet Levi got up,
left everything and followed him' (Luke 5:28).

The local Jews must have been staggered. Someone as flint-hearted
as Levi to leave it all—just like that! And then to immediately organize a kind of early 'Alpha course'—by inviting all his friends to dinner
to talk about Jesus…

It is so easy to forget that all we can see of people is their outer
shell. We can't know what is really going on in their hearts—how, no
matter what mean practices they apply, they may long to be otherwise.
How when the love and forgiveness of Jesus is presented to them
clearly, they may jump at it.

....

*Do you know someone whose
behaviour appals you? Have
they ever had a chance to consider Jesus Christ? How do you
know they wouldn't respond?*

Read Daniel 3 for another story
of how the most unlikely
people do respond to God.

AC

Back to basics

And beginning with Moses and all the Prophets, he explained to them what was said in all the Scriptures concerning himself… 'Were not our hearts burning within us while he… opened the Scriptures to us?'

Children's versions of Bible stories have a charm all their own—such as the following efforts:

'Adam and Eve were created from an apple tree.'
'Noah built an ark, which the animals came on to in pears.'
'Lot's wife was a pillar of salt by day, but a ball of fire by night.'

Such misunderstandings are funny, but many adults these days are pretty confused about the Bible, too. So how can they hope to grasp the relevance of Jesus for their lives? This encounter of Cleopas and his friend with Jesus on the road to Emmaus offers some tremendous pointers for anyone doing mission today.

Cleopas was still reeling from news of Jesus' crucifixion: he and his friend were grief-stricken. So why didn't Jesus simply say, 'Hey, it's me! I'm alive again!'? They would have been delighted—but even more bewildered. Instead, Jesus wanted them to *understand*. He wanted to reach their minds, not just their emotions. So he went back to basics, and patiently talked them through the whole amazing rescue plan God had set in motion with Moses all those centuries ago.

As the day wore on, Cleopas and his friend at last understood just where Jesus fitted into the picture. He was the Messiah; all Israelite history had looked forward to his coming. Then Cleopas and his friend looked again at Jesus, and at last recognized him for who he really was. Their joy was now all the deeper—for it was based on knowledge.

You could almost say the first 'Alpha Course' happened that day—people talking informally over just what Christianity is all about. There was an even an 'Alpha meal' at the end of it!

....

The Old Testament is a gripping read—and well worth the effort. Read just a chapter a day and you will get through it—promise!

AC

Sex and the City girl

'Therefore, I tell you, her many sins have been forgiven—for she loved much. But the one who has been forgiven little loves little.'

A friend asked me, 'Have many Christian women had too much sex? Whenever I'm with other Christians, and the subject of sex comes up, I wonder what they would say if they had any idea of what I used to do.' She laughed uneasily. 'Probably none of them would ever speak to me again.'

Not many women have a sexual record quite like the *Sex and the City* girls, but a great many past sexual encounters can haunt women. Mary Magdalene had had more men than she could remember: she had been a prostitute for years. All decent people in the town despised her. Mary was not 'respectable', and Mary, feeling the shame, would have kept out of their way.

Yet when she learned that Jesus was in town, she was not afraid to approach him. She crept into the house where he was dining, and offered him the most humble of services in the most beautiful of ways. In those days, washing a guest's feet was a common courtesy. But she washed his feet with her tears, kissed them, wiped them dry with her hair, and poured perfume on them.

It was her inarticulate way of begging for help. It was not sophisticated, but it was from the heart, with no excuses attached. And Jesus answered her heart-cry: 'Your sins are forgiven. Your faith has saved you; go in peace.'

His forgiveness gave her back her self-worth, her self-respect. She was whole again, and accepted by God. No wonder she could go in peace.

Whatever your past, it needn't haunt you. Jesus' love and forgiveness are real.

Read 2 Corinthians 5:16–21 and be assured that if anyone is in Christ, they are a new creation; the old has gone!

AC

Multi-tasking? No problem

And a woman was there who had been subject to bleeding for twelve years… When she heard about Jesus, she came up behind him in the crowd and touched his cloak, because she thought, 'If I just touch his clothes, I will be healed.' Immediately her bleeding stopped…

I have an agnostic friend who berates me every time I mention I have prayed about something personal. 'With all the suffering in the world, you should be praying about that,' he scoffs. 'God should be worrying about famine in Africa, not your x, y or z. You Christians are so self-centred.' The misery he sees in the world's headlines convinces him that God (if there is a God) should be doing something for the worst case scenarios, not for me. Until everyone else's worse problems are solved, I have no right to bring my small troubles to God.

So this story of the woman who was bleeding encourages me. Jesus was in the middle of answering a '999 call'—a little girl was dying, and the whole crowd was surging towards her home with Jesus in the forefront. They passed the woman who had been bleeding for twelve long years. There was nothing that had to happen *that morning* to keep her from actual death. But still she reached out to Jesus, intercepting him on his way to the critical situation.

And Jesus did not say to her, 'Do you mind? I'm male, and not into multi-tasking. One miracle at a time, or I'll get confused. Besides, your miracle is of lesser importance than the little girl.'

No. God is like the sun—radiating warmth and life all around. Any one of us can open our lives to him without him being diminished for anyone else. No one keeps their curtains shut so the sun will shine more on their garden.

So Jesus said, 'Daughter, your faith has healed you. Go in peace, and be freed from your suffering.' One woman's private discomfort—but Jesus had time and love enough to heal her.

....

Is there something wrong in your life that is weighing you down, making you miserable?

Read Philippians 4:4–9 for advice on what to do with those energy-sapping problems.

AC

He's not heavy, he's my brother

Since they could not get him to Jesus because of the crowd, they made an opening in the roof above Jesus and, after digging through it, lowered the mat the paralysed man was lying on. When Jesus saw their faith, he said to the paralytic, 'Son, your sins are forgiven.'

Imagine being in desperate need, and unable even to seek help. I know from bitter experience that paralysis can be mental as well as physical—we have someone in the family who suffers from depression.

What deeply moves me about this man's encounter with Jesus is the faithful persistence of his friends. He was in need, and they were going to get him to Jesus, no matter what effort it took. It was tough going. They got no cooperation from him; they had to carry him every inch of the way. (Have you ever prayed for someone who didn't want to know about Christ?) They got no help from the other followers of Jesus—in fact, the crowd was oblivious. (Where are other Christians when you need them?!) They had a wall to climb, and an obstacle to bash their way through. So they climbed and they bashed, and they hoisted their friend high, and lowered him down—right to Jesus' feet.

In all the other stories of encounters, Jesus responds to the faith of the individual concerned. Not here. This man didn't even have that! Instead, when Jesus saw *their* faith, he acted.

Do you know someone whose mental and spiritual need is paralysing their lives, who can't on their own make even the first step towards Jesus? Then, why not do as the friends did? Join with some Christians and, in persistent prayer, carry this person to Jesus.

The story concludes with Jesus bringing the man into a right relationship with himself, and healing him. At last the man was able to respond, and he immediately did two things: he praised God, and he stopped being a burden to others. He took up his mat, and with it, responsibility for himself. He was whole!

....

Is there someone in your past who carried you for a time? Thank God for them.

Read Galatians 6:1–10 for an insight into how we can help others spiritually.

AC

Persistent warrior or worrier?

[The centurion replied] 'For I myself am a man under authority, with soldiers under me. I tell this one, "Go", and he goes; and that one, "Come", and he comes...' When Jesus heard this, he was astonished and said to those following him, 'I tell you the truth, I have not found anyone in Israel with such great faith.'

Today is Remembrance Sunday. Today we honour the memory of the millions of brave soldiers who over the years have obeyed orders and gone into battle. They kept their vows to obey orders, even if it meant going to their death.

The centurion came from a harsh world. There was little compassion in the army of the Roman empire. But there was one thing in abundance—the use of authority. If someone high up in the Roman army decided something should happen, then that thing jolly well *did* happen. The centurion's world worked that way: some gave orders, and others obeyed orders. He'd heard of Jesus, and even at a distance he recognized the power of this man. For the centurion, power meant authority, which got things done. And so when he comes to Jesus, he shows his faith in the most natural way for a soldier: 'You are powerful, and if you command that this thing should happen, then it *will* happen.'

I am not in the army, but I do have two sorts of friends. Both kinds will occasionally say to me over some matter or other: 'Leave it with me, I'll deal with it.' Depending on which friend says it, I either feel confident the thing will most certainly get done, or else I get a sinking feeling, and know that is the last I will ever hear of it.

When I pray, I confess I sometimes treat Jesus as a scatter-brained friend. I bring him my troubles and explain them at great length. But I don't leave them with him. I keep going back and nudging him— 'Lord, you won't forget about...?' Persistent prayer is fine; persistent worry and doubt is quite another thing!

....

When you cast your cares on the Lord, it makes sense to leave them there. The centurion barely knew Jesus, but he did just that.

Philippians 4:4–7 is an encouragement to beat anxiety.

AC

84

Control freak

But Martha was distracted by all the preparations that had to be made. She came to him and asked, 'Lord, don't you care that my sister has left me to do the work by myself? Tell her to help me!'

Some women can be a menace, especially when they try to organize other women! Years ago, when we first moved to near Macclesfield, a woman at church discovered I loved Africa. The very next week a letter arrived from the diocesan committee on Black Anglican Concerns, welcoming me as the new secretary for the group. They were delighted, they said, that I could devote so much time to their work.

I was speechless. This woman had volunteered me!

Mary must have felt something like that on the day Jesus came. She was desperate to talk with him, and the story tells us she sat at his feet, like students did when they were learning from rabbis.

But then Martha comes in, bristling. Jesus has arrived, and she assumes he wants a meal. She responds to the apparent need in front of her. But does she have to do everything, she demands? Why isn't Mary helping her? Martha was what my aunt from Oklahoma would call 'a control freak'. She starts setting the agenda for everyone else around her, including Jesus, and getting herself into a frenzy.

Jesus' reply untangles her motives. 'Martha, Martha, you are worried and upset about many things, but *only one thing is needed*. Mary has chosen what is better, and it will not be taken away from her.'

Jesus had not laid any burden on Martha. He had not asked her to cook him a meal. In fact, while she was so busy doing what she assumed he required, she was actually *not* doing his will, which was to listen so he could teach her. As one Bible scholar has put it: 'Martha's concern was to be a proper hostess. Mary's was to be a proper disciple.'

....

There is a difference between doing our Father's business and religious busyness. If you are worried and anxious, who has laid all this on you?

Read Psalm 40 for an insight into how the psalmist found God's will for him.

AC

Treasure hunt

'Teacher, all these [commandments] I have kept since I was a boy.'
Jesus looked at him and loved him. 'One thing you lack,' he said.
'Go, sell everything you have and give to the poor, and you will have
treasure in heaven. Then come, follow me.'

You will have seen it in the films: two men are in the cave, fighting
over the gold treasure. But then the ceiling starts to collapse on them.
So the smart man leaves the treasure and runs for his life. The foolish
man tries to drag the gold out with him, and dies with it (think of the
Indiana Jones' films and *The Mummy*).

It happens in real life, too. One night my friend's grandfather's house
caught fire. He actually risked the flames to drag a small couch down
the stairs. Next morning he could not believe he had been so stupid. No
more stupid than those long-ago citizens of Pompeii who, with a vol-
cano blowing up beside them, tried to drag their goods away by cart.

Our attachment to our material wealth is quite incredible at times.
Material wealth can add a lot of enjoyment to life, but there are times
when it pays to let it go. It stops being useful when it becomes the
main focus of our lives.

Jesus' challenge to the young man was simple: what do you really
worship? Choose between me and your wealth. The young man
decided—and chose his wealth. So sadly, this story of an encounter
with Jesus ended in failure. The young man's wealth was so large and
important to him he failed to see the value of the one in front of him.

How do you feel about your material wealth? As Christians, we may
have to decide this question many times. Throughout our lives, we will
be faced with decisions on how to spend our money. There will be
times when we know God is asking us to give generously. If we do so,
we will not lose that wealth—we will simply be changing it into heavenly currency, and storing it up as treasure in heaven.

....

Why is it so easy to become too   Read Matthew 6:1–4 and 19–24
attached to the things we own?   for Jesus' advice on what to do
                                            with your material wealth.

                                                                    AC

Come down from your tree!

So [Zacchaeus] ran ahead and climbed a sycamore-fig tree to see him,
since Jesus was coming that way. When Jesus reached the spot, he
looked up and said to him, 'Zacchaeus, come down immediately. I
must stay at your house today.' So he came down at once, and welcomed him gladly.

Some years ago a man arrived late for a Billy Graham crusade. The main
doors were closed and guarded, because the arena was full. So the man
wandered upwards, staircase after staircase round the huge stadium. In
a quiet corridor, high up, he came across some Teddy Boys. He was so
disconsolate to find yet another door shut that one Teddy Boy obligingly
picked the lock for him. The Teddy Boys then followed the man in, and
together they looked down, down, down, at the tiny speck far below
that was Billy Graham. A little while later the man and the Teddy Boys
got 'up out of their seats', descended dozens of steps, and together
stood before Billy Graham, eager and glad to meet this Jesus.

   Zacchaeus wasn't a very 'likely prospect' for conversion either. His
past lifestyle had been one of sharp dealing, but in all the Gospel stories of encounters with Jesus, Zacchaeus was the only one whom Jesus
picked out from a crowd. Jesus simply asked for entry into his life, and
Zacchaeus was delighted. Having met Jesus, this chief tax collector
immediately decided to change some things in his life. Unlike the rich
young ruler who was serving his money, Zacchaeus decided to make his
money serve him. And so, 'Look, Lord! Here and now I give half of my
possessions to the poor, and if I have cheated anybody out of anything,
I will pay back four times the amount.' Jesus rejoiced that money had
lost its power over this man: 'Today salvation has come to this house…'

   It is wonderful to realize that Jesus actively seeks us out, as individuals. Zacchaeus is a challenging example of what a wholehearted
response to Jesus can be.

....

*Is there anything in your life that needs to be set right, restored, now
that Jesus has sought you out?*

                                                                    AC

An offer you can't refuse

Jesus answered, 'All who drink this water will be thirsty again, but those who drink the water I give them will never thirst. Indeed, the water I give them will become in them a spring of water welling up to eternal life.'

Getting the children to school on time. Getting to work on time. Shopping. Vacuuming. Ironing. Washing up. I haven't met many women with *time* to consider the meaning of life. They are glad the vicar is there for carol services and funerals, but they are content to leave him to it.

The woman of Samaria was the same. Her life consisted of daily chores, one thing after another. She wasn't against God: her people worshipped 'on this mountain', in contrast to the Jews worshipping in Jerusalem. But she was content to leave theological complications to the 'experts'.

She respected religious rules. When Jesus asked for water, she pointed out she was a Samaritan, whom the Jews saw as 'unclean'. She politely gave him a chance to draw back from her, but he did not.

Instead, this man talked more about water, but in a very confusing way! He said he had better water to offer her… then she realized he was talking about some refreshment in life that she was missing out on. It brought joy so intense, so personal, that once found it would refresh her whole being, continually—like a clear spring, bubbling up all on it own accord. Jesus explained that it was time for people to worship God directly, 'in sprit and in truth'. The Samaritan woman knew of a coming Messiah. 'I am he,' said Jesus.

In the middle of her small life, her daily chores, this woman found the Messiah personally offering her something nobody else could give her or take away: himself, *the water of life*. She, like us, was often physically exhausted by her daily routine. But her spirit need not be parched. The living water would become a spring in her, to eternal life.

....

It's not a matter of having to reach out to God all the time, it's Christ in us now that gives us hope of our future glory!

In Philippians 4:10–13 Paul shares his secret of coping with whatever life threw at him.

AC

Have to press on now

For me to live is Christ, and to die is gain.

I bought my little blue Skoda from a dealership whose owner is Christian. He rents a number of his secondhand cars out to missionaries back in this country on furlough. He charges about £5 a week.

One day my Skoda was in for a service, and I found the salesman was shaking his head in admiring bewilderment. 'We've just had one of those missionary ladies in here returning a car,' he said. 'She works with orphans in Papua New Guinea. A few weeks ago there was a riot in the town, and some men burned her house down. She lost everything, and nearly got killed. When I think of what that would do to my missus…' The man shook his head. 'But this lady didn't seem bothered. She seemed really happy, in fact—looking forward to getting back to the orphans… Amazing.' And he shook his head.

'For me to live is Christ, and to die is gain.' Over the past two weeks we have been looking at the impact Jesus had on individuals. Surely his effect on Paul was dramatic!

Paul had been on his way to persecute Christians when the risen Christ revealed himself to him on the Damascus Road. From that moment on, Paul was transformed. He had been a powerful Jew, well-respected and comfortably off. He ended up a despised Christian, imprisoned and beaten, often in want.

It didn't matter a fig to him. For now his only purpose in life was to be about his Father's business. And did he work! He became the apostle to the Gentiles, founding church after church, from Corinth to Galatia, Ephesus to Thessalonica. He fearlessly challenged religious and secular leaders alike. His letters form a great bulk of the New Testament. He changed the course of world history.

We can't all be like Paul, but what work is God calling you to do with your whole heart?

Read Hebrews 11 for a list of others who have responded wholeheartedly to God.

AC

Bugs and windshields

The jailer woke up, and when he saw the prison doors open, he drew his sword... to kill himself... But Paul shouted, 'Don't harm yourself! We are all here!'

The Americans have a saying: 'Sometimes you're the windshield, sometimes you're the bug.' It is shorthand for reminding you that in life sometimes you'll be caught at a disadvantage, but at other times you'll have the advantage over other people.

On this day in Acts, Paul had definitely been the bug. Uproar in the marketplace had ended in him and Silas being stripped and beaten, then fastened in stocks and locked away in a dark, noisy prison. How squashed can you get? Then that night—an earthquake. The prison doors are shaken loose, the chains fall off. The 'bugs' are free to limp away! When the jailer saw the prison doors open, that's what he figured had happened. He knew what the 'windscreen' of the Roman army would do to him for letting his prisoners go. Now he was the bug. In terror, he drew his sword to kill himself.

But Paul and Silas had not fled. The jailer had been callous towards their suffering, but they now showed him compassion and courtesy. Paul is concerned for the jailer. He is doing good to someone who has spitefully used him. 'Don't harm yourself!' he shouts. The jailer was speechless. Prisoners whom he had mistreated were now showing him mercy and consideration. 'The jailer called for lights, rushed in and fell trembling before Paul and Silas. He then brought them out and asked "Sirs, what must I do to be saved?"' *Sirs*, no less!

In this last of our Gospel encounters with Christ, Christ is not physically present to meet the jailer. But Paul radiates Christ's spirit of compassion. And the jailer and all his household gladly respond.

And so the 'bugs' win the day, without having to turn into the windscreen. No one gets smashed.

....

Is there someone who has hurt you, to whom you could show kindness and mercy? Think what might happen then!

Read Matthew 5:38–42 for Jesus' advice on what to do when you are mistreated.

AC

Trusting God for completeness

Meeting Jesus transforms lives, as Anne Coomes has highlighted. And that transformation does not depend on outward circumstances or even on how we feel. Often our feelings are out of step with the reality that in Christ we are made new: 'the old has gone, the new has come!' (2 Corinthians 5:17).

When I first began to plan this series of notes, Jennifer Rees Larcombe was to have written the next set focusing on what it means to be complete people. I first met Jen 20 years ago when she was virtually bedridden, suffering from a rare viral disease that threatened her life. After eight years, miraculously, God healed her and has faithfully led her through many other difficulties—the reason she was unable to write these notes was because a grandchild was facing a major operation and the family needed support.

Jen now leads the charity *Beauty from Ashes*, which aims to encourage people whose lives have been distorted or broken through loss and trauma. Jen and her team encourage broken people towards faith in, and dependence on, Christ.

For Jen, and for all of us who know Jesus, being complete is a gift from God. It's a reality that has nothing to do with our own efforts, success, health or circumstances. But sometimes it needs a firm decision on our part to trust God, whatever we have to face.

We will all face difficulties in this life. You might be facing serious challenges right now. Find that most familiar of Psalms, Psalm 23 and remind yourself of the security you have in Christ. If you seem to be walking through 'green pastures' right now, make a firm decision to trust God—even when those feelings change. Then when you are walking through 'Death Valley', which you will, where the light of Christ is like a dim glimmer at the end of a shadowy tunnel, then you can stand firm, because you have already decided to trust God, not feelings or fate.

Impossibly perfect

'Be perfect, therefore, as your heavenly Father is perfect.'

Driving through Romania at the end of the oppressive Ceausescu era, the pop song *Shiny Happy People* by chart band REM seemed a perfect way to describe the Romanian Christians we met. Although the shops only seemed to stock jars of pickled vegetables, electricity supplies to homes were intermittent, and poverty seemed one of life's few certainties, the people we met shone with love for God and each other. They seemed to embody Jesus' words in this passage: they were the salt of the earth; light in a dark world.

Returning home to our easy English lifestyle, with shops brimming with Christmas gifts, where freedom, well-paid work, warm homes and good food are often taken for granted, why do so many of us seem to be depressed, grumpy people? Like many of the world's poor or persecuted believers, these 'shiny happy' Christians know the blessing of God and that makes their lives complete. Yes, they experience hardship, pain, conflict and injustice, and they are working hard to make a difference in their communities. But whether or not they succeed in human terms, their happiness does not depend on life's circumstances.

When Jesus met a rich young man (Matthew 19:18–22) who wanted eternal life, Jesus reminded him about the law—just as he does in today's reading, ending with the seemingly impossible challenge to be perfect. The young man went away sad 'because he had great wealth'. Jesus was pinpointing the man's heart attitude. He kept the law, but not necessarily because he loved God. His possessions were his first love.

But isn't the Christian life about grace? I can't possibly be perfect, so why does Jesus underline God's legal requirement for righteous perfection? In the next two weeks we will be trying to see our lives from God's perspective, aiming to discover how we can be perfect, complete in his sight.

....

Father, help me to know my own heart and to see myself as you see me.

Do read Matthew 19:18–22, the story of the rich young man.

CFB

Perfectly acceptable

The law is only a shadow of the good things that are coming… it can never, by the same sacrifices repeated endlessly year after year, make perfect those who draw near to worship… we have been made holy through the sacrifice of the body of Jesus Christ once for all…

I am not a brilliant baker, so I identified closely with the character played by Helen Mirren in the film *Calendar Girls* when she won a WI baking competition with a shop-bought cake. Her entry had achieved the standard the judges required—but she had played no part in achieving the desired results. The judges' standards for perfection would have highlighted the imperfections of a home-made offering.

Similarly, the Old Testament law sets a standard that highlights our imperfections—especially when Jesus explains that even looking at someone lustfully is as bad as committing adultery. I can never achieve the standard set by the law, but Jesus gave his life to fulfil God's requirement for justice, which balances his love. I play no part in achieving God's standard. All I need to do is accept Jesus' gift of life in him.

Before Jesus came, the temple system of priests and sacrifices reminded people that their shortcomings needed to be cancelled out. That's why they sacrificed animals. Jesus brought an end to the system by becoming the once-for-all sacrifice. Only Jesus is qualified to cancel our shortcomings, because his sinless life perfectly fulfilled every aspect of the law. As Hebrews 4:15 says, 'We do not have a high priest who is unable to sympathize with our weaknesses, but we have one who has been tempted in every way, just as we are—yet was without sin.'

Now perfection is possible for us, too. We become perfect in God's sight when we accept Jesus' sacrifice on our behalf: 'by one sacrifice he has made perfect forever those who are being made holy' (Hebrews 10:14). Although we are still becoming holy, God sees us as perfect if we are covered by Jesus' perfection.

....

Father, thank you that you loved me so much, you gave Jesus as the once-for-all sacrifice, making it possible for me to get to know you.

Read Romans 3:21–26 for Paul's comparison between law and grace.

CFB

Love is blind

He chose us in him before the creation of the world to be holy and blameless in his sight. In love he predestined us to be adopted as his children through Jesus Christ, in accordance with his pleasure and will—to the praise of his glorious grace, which he has freely given us in the One he loves.

Love is blind, the saying goes. This idealistic love takes no notice of the beloved's imperfection. But modern romances seem more realistic: the fictional Bridget Jones is all too aware of her suitors' flaws.

But Paul's letter to the Ephesians reminds us that God's love for those who are in Christ is blind to our guilt and blame. He sees us as holy and blameless. The crucial word in today's reading is 'in'. If we are *in* Christ we are 'holy and blameless'; he freely gives us his glorious grace if we are *in* the One he loves; '*in* him we have redemption … forgiveness of sins… *in* him we were also chosen…' and we were marked '*in* him with a seal, the promised Holy Spirit, who is a deposit guaranteeing our inheritance'.

If we are 'in Christ' we have a new life that entitles us to all the blessings and riches God reserves for his precious children. God's love for us does not alter because of what we do or don't do for him. He loves us because we have been adopted as his children. We have taken on a new identity.

Being 'in Christ' means we have a new spiritual DNA that marks us out as part of God's family: 'The Spirit himself testifies with our spirit that we are God's children' (Romans 8:16). We may not yet be holy in all we do, but part of the Holy Spirit's work is to reveal Jesus to us and to teach us how to live. We become more holy as we respond to his love.

Make Ephesians 1:18–21 a personal prayer today, then make these verses a prayer for a friend or relative.

Read 1 Corinthians 13:4–8a to remind yourself how God loves you.

CFB

Motivated by love

We know that we live in him and he in us, because he has given us of his Spirit. And we have seen and testify that the Father has sent his Son to be the Saviour of the world. If any acknowledge that Jesus is the Son of God, God lives in them and they in God.

Thinking about light and colour helps me grasp something of God's mystery as the Trinity. The light we can see may seem colourless, but the basic colours of red, blue and green are always present. What seemed to be one colour, is in fact three.

Our limited minds find it difficult to understand the individuality yet intimate unity of the Trinity. It is not easy to hold in tension the fact that God is one, yet three-in-one. But God the Father, God the Son and God the Holy Spirit are all involved in the family relationship that allows us to be perfect and complete in God's sight as this reading shows.

So how does God show that he loves us? 'He sent his one and only Son into the world that we might live through him' (v. 9). When God the Father sent Jesus to take the punishment we deserve, he was not acting as a cosmic child-abuser, separated from the suffering of the Son. The Father, Son and Holy Spirit are one. God gave himself for us because he loves us: 'This is love: not that we loved God, but that he loved us and sent his Son as an atoning sacrifice for our sins' (v. 10).

Love is the motive behind God's rescue plan for humanity. But he can't let wrong go unpunished. We would be the first to cry: 'That's not fair!' if wrong-doing was ignored.

But God can hold justice and love in perfect balance. Justice is satisfied when love pays the penalty for our sin.

See, from his head, his hands, his feet, sorrow and love flow mingled down...

Isaac Watts (1674–1748)

Remember, you have stolen God's heart. Read Song of Songs 4:9.

CFB

Lavish love

What marvellous love the Father has extended to us! Just look at it—we're called children of God! That's who we really are.

Because I love my children, I want them to know there are consequences if they cross the boundaries I have given them: boundaries like 'Don't go near the fire—you'll be burned!'; 'Don't walk in front of fast cars—you'll be killed!'; and more subtle boundaries like 'Don't tell lies—you'll destroy trust'. I hope my children will stay within the boundaries because they love me and are confident of my love for them. I'd prefer a response out of love to compliance motivated by fear of fire, fast cars or my anger!

God is also looking for a response of love, but so often we want rules rather than the loving relationship he has in mind. It seems so much easier to live by a list of dos and don'ts rather than developing an intimate relationship with God and learning to obey him because we love him.

But what's the difference in the end? You might ask. Surely the outcome is the same? But it's not. When religious people set rules for living, those rules don't make people better—they simply highlight failure and offer no power to change.

As I fell in love with my husband I wanted to please him; nothing seemed too difficult to face. In the heat of first love, even otherwise boring football matches seemed bearable! I simply wanted to be with the one I loved and to enjoy what he enjoyed. But if he had said, 'You *must* watch every match' that law would have made me a slave to football, highlighting my lack of enthusiasm for the game.

On a less trivial level, I want to do what is right because I love God, not just because I'm doing what I'm told. But, even if I fail, God's lavish love for me does not change. He loves me because I am *in Christ*, not because of how I behave. In his eyes, I'm perfect, because of Jesus.

....

Ask God to show you any area of your life where you are living by man-made rules, rather than being motivated by God's love.

Read John 15:9–17 to see Jesus' own words on the centrality of love.

CFB

Mismatch?

Consider it pure joy, my brothers and sisters, whenever you face trials of many kinds, because you know that the testing of your faith develops perseverance. Perseverance must finish its work so that you may be mature and complete, not lacking anything.

The readings in these last few days have highlighted the fact that, because we are *in Christ*, we are perfect in God's sight—loved by God and blessed with every spiritual blessing. But we don't always match up to our own expectations, never mind God's perfect standard. Also, life doesn't always seem as if we're being blessed. Why the mismatch?

Life's difficulties offer us a choice: to focus on the problem or to focus on what we know to be true about God. In the Psalms, David's change of attitude is often noticeable: Psalms 13 and 43 both show a remarkable change of focus. They start with David bemoaning his sorry state. Then he realizes who he is and who he is serving. He reminds himself what God is like: 'But I trust in your unfailing love; my heart rejoices in your salvation. I will sing to the Lord, for he has been good to me' (Psalm 13:5–6).

As he focuses on what he knows to be true about God, his problems take on a different perspective. In this reading James is typically practical about what it means to be complete and faultless—our responses, words and actions show if we are taking God's words seriously. But he puts rules and regulations in their place, describing the law as a mirror that shows us what we are like. Looking at the law's rules we see we are failures. Looking at God and his lavish love, we can respond with grateful hearts, certain that whatever life throws at us, God is at work to make us mature and complete. Difficulty can be embraced with joy because it is part of God's refining process.

....

Father, hear the prayer we offer! Not for ease that prayer shall be,
But for strength that we may ever live our lives courageously.

Love Maria Willis (1824–1908)

CFB

Secure and at peace

Therefore, since we have been justified through faith, we have peace with God through our Lord Jesus Christ… And we rejoice in the hope of the glory of God. Not only so, but we also rejoice in our sufferings, because we know that suffering produces perseverance; perseverance, character; and character, hope.

'Therefore' is frequently used in Paul's letter to the Romans as he sets out God's rescue plan. He arrives at this 'therefore' having explained to his readers about humanity's sinfulness, God's judgment, God's faithfulness and the forgiveness available through Jesus. He then gives the example of Abraham who was right with God not because of any rituals or religious practices, but because he believed God and trusted him to fulfil his promise.

I grew up at a time when Christians were often marked by the rules they obeyed: Christians don't dance, don't drink alcohol, don't wear short skirts… It was possible to look very religious without ever having a change of heart. But Paul reminds us that peace with God has nothing to do with what we do, what we wear or where we go. We can't earn peace with God. It's a gift, given to us 'while we were still sinners'. It doesn't depend on our churchgoing or Bible reading, eloquent praying or sacrificial giving, charity work or work for the church.

Peace with God doesn't depend on how we feel, either. The fact that Jesus has rescued us and has brought us into an eternal relationship with God is worth celebrating—even when life's journey takes us through suffering. Some of the most serene and peaceful people I know are those who face daily difficulties, but have settled in their hearts that God is good and has their best interests at heart. They know they are valuable to God—worth sending his Son to die for. Their self-worth doesn't depend on their standing in society or their achievements, their health or wealth. Where do your peace and security lie?

....

Father, help me to rest and to rejoice in the knowledge that you have done everything necessary for me to have peace with you.

                                                                        CFB

Life in the Spirit

Therefore, there is now no condemnation for those who are in Christ Jesus… if the Spirit of him who raised Jesus from the dead is living in you, he who raised Christ from the dead will also give life to your mortal bodies through his Spirit, who lives in you.

When friends adopted a baby, there were no signs of anything unusual until they noticed he wasn't developing as he should. As they discovered more about his background, they found his siblings had the same severe mental handicaps. No matter how loving and accepting adoptive parents are, human adoption can't change a child's genetic make-up.

Being adopted into God's family is quite different. Jesus substitutes his life-giving Spirit for our sinful nature. Outside of Christ our lives are condemned to the consequences of our sin. In Christ, his Spirit gives us life, along with all the privileges and responsibilities of being part of God's family. The Holy Spirit comes to live with us, leading us and reminding us of God's truth.

We have no need to live fearful, condemned lives, like prisoners on death row. We have been set free to enjoy an intimate, loving relationship with our Father God. As the hymn 'Man of sorrows' says, 'In my place condemned he stood; Sealed my pardon with His blood' (Philip Bliss, 1838–76).

Ask God to speak to you throughout the day. Take time to listen to the whispers of God's Spirit. And this evening, as you reflect on the places you have been and the people you have met, ask God 'Where were you in that place?', 'What were you saying when I met that person?' Sometimes the Holy Spirit points out something wrong in what we've said or done. Deal with it quickly, asking God's forgiveness and putting it right with anyone else who has been affected. Then, as in Hebrews 10:19–22, enter God's presence with confidence. He has made the way clear.

....

Use Matthew 6:9–13 as a pattern for prayer.

CFB

Why does God allow suffering?

I consider that our present sufferings are not worth comparing with the glory that will be revealed in us. The creation waits in eager expectation for the sons of God to be revealed.

Suffering that has an end in sight and a reward is somehow more bearable than unending days and nights of discomfort. A marathon runner or mountaineer presses through the pain barrier to achieve his or her goal. For mothers-to-be in labour, the discomfort (some might say agony) is made more bearable by the hope that it will be over soon and there will be a baby as a result.

Christians also live in the hope that this world is only the beginning of eternal life with God. We have our hopes set on the future and that helps to make our present difficulties more bearable. Jesus described the world's suffering—war, famine, earthquakes—as birth pains (Matthew 24:4–8). He also said his followers would be persecuted and even put to death.

For some believers, suffering and persecution for their faith is a present reality. In *The Heavenly Man* (Monarch Books, 2002), Chinese Christian Brother Yun describes the persecution suffered today by Chinese Christians. He writes:

Christians who are in prison for the sake of the Lord are not the ones who are suffering. When people hear my testimony they often say 'You must have had a terrible time when you were in prison.' I respond, 'What are you talking about? I was with Jesus and had overwhelming joy and peace in his intimate presence.'

The people who really suffer are those who never experience God's presence. The way to have God's presence is by walking through hardship and suffering—the way of the cross…

....

Read John 10:27–29 and thank God for his presence and help in your life.

CFB

Nothing is wasted

If God is on our side, can anyone be against us? God did not keep back his own Son, but he gave him for us. If God did this, won't he freely give us everything else? If God says his chosen ones are acceptable to him, can anyone... condemn them?

Do you ever look back amazed at how God has been at work at different times in your life: before you became a Christian he was talking to you through different circumstances and the people you met; as you have drawn closer to him, he has been teaching you more about himself through the joys and challenges you have faced. No experience has been wasted, although we may have to wait until we see him face to face to understand why he has allowed some things to happen in our lives.

The apostle Paul knew from his own life that God does not waste any experience. God weaves all our past and present into the future he is preparing for us. Before Paul encountered Christ on the Damascus road, he was very religious. He was a Pharisee who persecuted Christians, trained by Gamaliel, a celebrated doctor of Jewish law. Once God turned his life around, Paul put all his training to good use, explaining God's rescue plan for humanity and how Jesus cancels the requirements of the law. He travelled throughout the known world on three major missionary journeys. But he also spent time in prison and put that time to good use, writing letters to various churches. Without his time in captivity, we would probably have had very little of the New Testament.

Paul was convinced that God had his best interest at heart. With the creator of the universe on his side, he knew no enemy could defeat him. If you feel that God is against you, you could become angry and resentful when bad things happen. But if, like Paul, you know that God wants the best for you, then every obstacle becomes an opportunity to discover God's grace and power at work in your life.

Ask God to help you to trust that he is at work in all of life's circumstances.

Read Jeremiah 29:11–14 for reassurance about God's plans for you.

CFB

All you need is love

Who shall separate us from the love of Christ?... I am convinced that neither death nor life, neither angels nor demons, neither the presen nor the future, nor any powers, neither height nor depth, nor any thing else in all creation, will be able to separate us from the love o God that is in Christ Jesus our Lord.

Is love all you need? Psychologist Pepper Schwartz says that the cupid love, so idolized by our society, may be 'a great elixir, but making commitment based on hormone-addled logic is a recipe for disappoint ment, if not disaster' (*Psychology Today*, Sussex Publishers, New York 2002).

Schwartz says relationships work when both partners are good lis teners; able to understand how the other feels; able to think easily o things to do together; creative in handling differences; willing to make adjustments in the relationship. These qualities may not be what we first think of when we talk of love, but aren't they at the heart of deep lasting love?

How does the psychologist's description of a good relationship com pare with the relationship between you and Jesus? Jesus made the mas sive adjustment of leaving heaven for earth, taking on all the limitation of our humanity, our weaknesses and temptations. Our independen spirits make us so different from him—Jesus only does what he sees hi Father doing. But Jesus dealt with this fundamental difference by givin us his Spirit, changing us from the inside and revealing himself to us That's certainly a creative way to handle such a massive difference.

Jesus longs to develop an intimate relationship with you; to be the one who listens to you. He understands how you feel and he enjoy your company. Nothing can separate you from his love. He also want you to listen to him; to hear him say how much he loves you; to enjo his company; to be aware of his companionship in everything you do

....

Ask God to help you to be more   Read Song of Solomon 8:6–7 fo
aware of his presence in every   a description of passionate love.
aspect of your life.   CF

Beauty and the Beast

I always thank God for you… in him you have been enriched in every way… you do not lack any spiritual gift as you eagerly wait for our Lord Jesus Christ to be revealed. He will keep you strong to the end, so that you will be blameless on the day of our Lord Jesus Christ.

It is crucial to the tale of 'Beauty and the Beast' that Beauty falls in love with the Beast before he is transformed into a handsome prince. Love sees potential as well as present reality. In the romance between us and God, we had already won God's heart while we were sinners (Romans 5:8).

When Paul writes to the church at Corinth he is full of gratitude to God, love for the Corinthians and hope for their future. He sees them as God sees them—enriched in every way, not lacking any spiritual gift, strong, and with the prospect of being blameless when they come face to face with God at the end of time. Paul sees them as perfect but being made holy (Hebrews 10:14); his emphasis is fully on what God has done for them *in Christ*. His ability to describe the Corinthians as 'blameless' and 'not lacking' is all the more remarkable as we read through Paul's letter, which tackles division and disorder in the church, lawsuits among believers and inappropriate behaviour in worship and at the Lord's Supper.

At the heart of the letter, Paul puts all their squabbling and bad behaviour into the context of love. He reminds them that 'Love is patient, love is kind. It does not envy, it does not boast, it is not proud. It is not rude, it is not self-seeking, it is not easily angered, it keeps no record of wrongs. Love does not delight in evil but rejoices with the truth' (1 Corinthians 13:4–6).

Paul is challenging them to change their behaviour towards one another, but his letter also reminds us how God's love can see us, *in Christ*, as 'blameless'—because he loves us, his Son's perfect bride.

....

Thank you, Father God, for being patient with me, protecting me, persevering with me. Thank you that you keep no record of my wrongs.

Read 2 Peter 1:3–4 for more assurance about God's full provision of spiritual gifts.

CFB

When the veil is removed

We, who with unveiled faces all reflect the Lord's glory, are being transformed into his likeness with ever-increasing glory, which comes from the Lord, who is the Spirit.

Have you ever taken a friend on a course introducing people to Christian faith? Some questions seem so important. What about other faiths? Why does God allow suffering? What does the Bible say about sex? It can be as if there's a brick wall between your friend and Jesus. If only she could experience the love of God and his power, you know the questions would be resolved—not because they have easy answers, but because having a relationship with Jesus makes all the difference.

I do not need to know all the answers when I know the person who does. Maybe that's why Jesus said we need to come to him like little children (Matthew 18:3). A child who is secure and confident in her parents' love doesn't need to worry about what's going to happen tomorrow; she can simply enjoy today, safe in the knowledge that her parents have it all worked out. That trust can put human parents under pressure, because they know their resources are limited. But God's resources are limitless and he delights to give good gifts to his children (Matthew 7:11).

It is an amazing privilege to be with someone when the brick wall of unbelief comes crashing down and she comes face to face with Jesus. It's as if she were blind, but now she can see; as if a veil over her face has been taken away. Once we are part of God's family, we can still bring our concerns for those who don't recognize Jesus or who suffer; we can still ask him about life's big moral questions and how we can live in line with our Maker's instructions. But a transformation has taken place. We are not living by a set of rules, but we are enjoying a relationship—responding to God's lavish love. And that's what changes us. The more we get to know him, the more we become like him.

....

Jesus, change me. May your Holy Spirit get to work transforming me to be more and more like you.

Read about one family's transformation in Acts 16:16–34.

CFB

Everything necessary

His divine power has given us everything we need for life and godliness through our knowledge of him who called us by his own glory and goodness. Through these he has given us his very great and precious promises, so that through them you may participate in the divine nature.

If you've been following the notes over the past few weeks, you'll know that it is possible to be perfect in God's sight; not because of what you do or don't do, but because you are adopted into God's family through Jesus. Through the cross, God has done everything necessary to make your life complete.

If there's nothing we can do to make ourselves more pleasing to God, we might find ourselves repeating Paul's question: shall we go on sinning so God can keep forgiving (Romans 6:1)? Of course not! If I have been genuinely captivated by God's love, I want to live to please him. He has given me his divine nature: his Spirit who works in me to produce good fruit. Now I can live an effective and productive life.

As a child in Sunday school I used to sing an old chorus: 'Standing on the promises I cannot fall, Listening every moment to the Spirit's call, Resting in my Saviour as my all in all, Standing on the promises of God' (Russell Kelso Carter, 1849–1928). As a child, I didn't know many of God's promises and I certainly hadn't put them to the test. Now, with the hindsight of years, I know that God speaks the truth when he says he has given me everything I need.

Christians used to use a 'promise box' to pick out a text for the day—like sanctified astrology. I'm not suggesting thumbing through the Bible to pick out a few choice texts—but what promises has the Holy Spirit underlined in your heart, verses you know to be God's word to you? Write them down. Chew on them as you walk about and let the truth of God's promises shape your words, actions and feelings.

....

Father, help me to walk through today seeing my life through your eyes. Human sight is so unreliable. I need to see life from your perspective.

Read Colossians 3:1–17 for a further challenge to life and godliness.

CFB

105

Longing for home

Getting to grips with what the Bible says is always a challenge to me as a writer: am I living what I write? Sometimes I can identify closely with the poet John Donne who challenged God to be like a blacksmith, hammering his heart into shape.

Batter my heart, three-person'd God; for you
As yet but knock; breathe, shine, and seek to mend;
That I may rise, and stand, o'erthrow me, and bend
Your force, to break, blow, burn, and make me new.
I, like an usurp'd town, to another due,
Labour to admit you, but O, to no end.

Like Donne, my life doesn't just need a light polish—it needs completely reshaping. I know in my head that he is loving and trustworthy, faithful and generous; that he has adopted me into his family and has lifted me up, giving me full access to his presence. But I don't always live as if my heart believes what my head knows.

At the hardest times—facing illness, broken relationships or the separation that death brings—I have known God wrapping his arms around me, almost tangibly. But at other times, it is as if I let my guard slip. I take my eyes off Jesus and began to rely on my own efforts, or the support of others. That's when I need God to knock me back into shape. Sometimes I need to be tough on myself, but from time to time, like the disciples with Jesus, I need to step out of the busyness of life—to take time out to refocus and be refreshed.

How about you? Do you need to take a firm grip on yourself and decide to trust God, even though life seems tough right now? Or do you need time out with God?

In the next two weeks Bridget Plass will be looking at homes in the Bible. When God said he had 'set eternity in the human heart' (Ecclesiastes 3:11), perhaps he meant he has given us all a longing for home; the type of home where we can be ourselves; a safe place if some major work needs to be done on the foundations of our lives.

Homesickness

The Lord God put the man in the Garden of Eden to take care of it… Late in the afternoon… the man and the woman heard the Lord God walking in the garden.

What do you miss most about home when you are away? I think it's the ritual of making my first cup of tea in the morning when no one else is up and no one needs me to do anything and I can just be. First I potter about the kitchen making my tea in my favourite mug. In the summer I meander into the back garden and enjoy the peace and early morning smells. In the winter I snuggle into an armchair. My special time. Tea made from a hotel's 'tea and coffee making facilities' never quite hits the same spot.

For my husband, it is the routine of walking the dog in the afternoon. For the dog, ditto! And for the first Adam it was his walk with God in the cool of the late afternoon. His exile meant an end to this intimate special time, to everything familiar and cosy, which he had not necessarily appreciated at the time. As the gates to his home were barred to him forever, he must have yearned more than anything for those special times, familiar routines and comforting rituals that make up life at home.

The whole of the Bible is the story of humanity's futile attempts to get back to that place of security with God. Homesick for something we do not understand, we strive to find a way back. Until Jesus dies and the gates to home are flung wide open again. And there, Jesus tells us is a place for each one of us. Not cold and impersonal places with 'tea and coffee making facilities', but homes prepared especially for us. And maybe we will be able to walk with God in the cool of the afternoon.

What do you miss most when you are way from your home? Thank God for just that today.

Read John 14:2–4 for the promise Jesus made about our future homes.

BP

Fathering: to speak or not to speak

Job's sons took turns having feasts in their homes, and always invited their three sisters. After each feast, Job would send for his children and perform a ceremony, as a way of asking God to forgive them for any wrongs they might have done. He would get up early the next morning, and offer a sacrifice for each of them, just in case they had sinned.

If Job was the very best God-fearing man Satan could find to tempt, then the way he ran his house must have been pretty good too. So it's worth a look.

Do you know I really love the picture conveyed here. He has fathered a close loving family who enjoy nothing better than getting together in one of their homes for a meal and some drinks. This must mean that feasting together, laughing and talking, featured strongly while they were growing up.

But now they are adult will they manage to control themselves? Will they do something silly after a few drinks? Those of us with adult children can sympathize with old worry-guts Job, but I can't help wondering what his family felt about always having to pop over to dad's for a forgiveness ceremony after a good night's party. The fact they went shows their respect for him.

I think the bit I like best in this passage is that he loves them so much he prefers to get up early every morning and pray for them rather than constantly argue about what is making them happy.

I have decided that as children grow through teenage there is an increasing need to keep your mouth shut and pray hard! Perhaps that should apply to everyone close to us. Shut up and pray hard!!

....

Dear Father, help us with all our dealings with those we love to be as wise and thorough as Job.

Read Ecclesiastes 3:1–14 and think what the writer means when he says that God has 'set eternity in the human heart'.

BP

It's not fair

Why do evil people live so long and gain such power?... They have
no worries at home, and God never punishes them. Their cattle have
lots of calves without losing one; their children play and dance
safely by themselves... and they are successful, without a worry,
until the day they die... What do we gain from worshipping you?

Oops. Only the other day I caught myself having exactly this sort of
bitter fury moment about a non-Christian family who seem to sail
through life extremely happily without a solitary moment of guilt
about their total disregard of God. They have a gorgeous house, successful kids, no money worries or health problems and it is easy to
have a 'why God?' moment when you are up to your eyes in yet
another crisis. We are not even allowed to feel smug that they will
get their come-uppance when they die, because we are supposed to
be praying for their salvation!

Judging from Job's sentiments expressed here, clearly 'keeping up
with the Jones' is not a new concept but what is it that makes a display of material wealth something we covet so highly? Is it that it is
a visible sign of success, of being someone special, of having arrived?
Is it simply that having nice things is very nice? Or maybe we are
all tempted to judge ourselves by how much we or our children
achieve. Again, I have to remind myself that all that really counts is
what we are left with when the house built on poor foundations
collapses.

What do we gain from worshipping God? A peace the world cannot give? Well, sometimes. Hope? The knowledge we are forgiven
and safe? Like all the best things in life, such as love, it's hard to
define. All I know is that I would be infinitely poorer without God in
my life. How about you?

....

Dear Father, help us to be
aware of all you have put into
our lives, which has survived
whatever storms have come.

Read Philippians 3:7–15 to discover what Paul felt God had
replaced his old values with.

BP

The best sort of hostess

Once, while Elisha was in the town of Shunem, he met a rich woman who invited him to her home for dinner. After that, whenever he was in Shunem, he would have a meal with her and her husband. Some time later the woman said to her husband, 'I'm sure the man who comes here so often is a prophet of God. Why don't we build him a small room on the flat roof of our house? We can put a bed, a table and a chair, and an oil lamp in it. Then whenever he comes he can stay with us.'

What a wise and truly generous woman the rich woman of Shunem was. She was not thinking about how she could parade her famous visitor about, not even looking forward to meals during which she might hear more of God. She was only thinking about what he would like. She must have sensed how weary he felt and how he yearned for the occasional day off from being a prophet of God! Her generosity was not the provision of the bed, the table and the lamp—she could probably easily afford them. Her generosity sprang from putting herself in his shoes and providing what he needed—a little bolt hole, his own space.

A while ago, after almost all my children had left home, I had a spare room, a proper guest room. I put a little sink in it, and new white bedlinen and fluffy towels. Small though it was, it looked very pretty, almost like a room in a magazine. Adrian wanted to add books and a TV and a comfy chair—homely things. I wanted it to remain pristine and perfect. Why? So visitors had to worry about what they might spoil? So they would not feel comfortable enough to stay in it except to lie carefully and neatly on the bed? Adrian was right. So was the woman of Shunem. Reading this story again has made me hope that next time we have visitors I will try to be more sensitive to their needs at that particular time, and think more carefully about what they actually want rather than what I want and need from their company.

....

Dear Father, show me how to be
sensitive to the needs of those
who come to my home. Help
me to respond to their agenda.

Read about Jesus' bolt hole, the place he could be himself among friends, in Luke 10:38–42.

BP

Behind closed doors

Potiphar liked Joseph and made him his personal assistant, putting him in charge of his house and all his property… Joseph was well-built and handsome, and Potiphar's wife soon noticed him. She asked him to make love to her… she kept begging Joseph day after day, but he refused to do what she wanted or even to go near to her.

The worst abuse always happens behind closed doors. Often in the home. Sometimes it goes on for a very long time undetected. Almost always the victim is made to feel it is their fault despite being powerless to stop it.

Joseph may have been an adult, but as a slave he was utterly powerless as he soon discovered when Potiphar's rejected wife stitched him up with lies and he ended up in prison. It wasn't his fault. It never is the fault of the powerless when they are abused in any way. Abuse can take many forms. Bullying, neglect, ridicule can seem part of normal family life, but for some they can distort personality as much as the more obvious sexual and physical forms.

And we are told it is one of the things that makes God angry. When little ones are made to stumble in whatever way, God is angry.

The great lesson of this story has to be that even behind closed doors God knows what is going on. It may feel at the time as though he does nothing, but Joseph's story is one of hope. God was with him here and in prison. He never left him and he never stopped loving him; later in life Joseph was able to see that for himself. But for now he had to hang on… Sometimes things that happen to you in the home, behind closed doors, are so bad you can feel God can't bear to look at you. But he is looking at you, loving you, wanting to take your guilt and your shame and show you it is not your fault.

Dear Father, help me today. If I have been abused restore my sense of being beautiful in your eyes. If I have abused in any way, forgive me. If I need help, give me the courage to seek it.

BP

Home from home

David and his men were hiding at the back of the cave. They whispered to David, 'The Lord told you he was going to let you defeat your enemies… This must be the day.'

Many years ago Adrian and I took our family camping at one of the big Christian festivals. It poured with rain for the whole three days we were there and all our children turned into mud cakes. Our tent became a mud tent. But it was great fun. What was not very fun was the fact that every night, from about two in the morning till three, the inhabitants of several tents near us saw fit to have a communal singsong. Now it may have been a very Spirit-led singsong. One tent would begin a chorus and the next tent would join in, energetically and loudly praising the Lord. It probably blessed them greatly. Not so our tent. Our children would all wake up and not get back to sleep again until long after the surrounding noise eventually subsided. Now I usually pride myself on being a very tolerant person. Not this time. My excuse is that three grumpy, tired mud cakes are absolutely ghastly!

What I think puzzled me was that when we met the inhabitants of these tents, they turned out to be ultra-respectable types—far more respectable than us! Yet they had happily abandoned all the natural courtesy they would no doubt extend at home.

At the time of the famous incident of Saul, in American-speak, 'going to the bathroom' in the cave in which David has taken refuge, David was far from home. Cut off from everything familiar, exhausted by the strain of being constantly afraid, it would not have surprised anyone if he had given in to the temptation presented to him. But for David, at least at this stage in his life, the fact that he was living this nomadic existence did not mean he felt able to abandon all he had been taught when he had a more permanent residence. 'He's my king, and I pray that the Lord will keep me from doing anything to harm his chosen king' (v. 7).

....

Father, help me to hold on to all you have taught me about caring for others, even when my routine's interrupted or I'm away from home.

BP

When the cupboard is bare

Elijah... saw a widow gathering sticks for a fire... he asked, 'Would you also please bring me a piece of bread?' The widow answered, '... I swear that I don't have any bread. All I have is a handful of flour and a little olive oil. I'm on my way home now with these few sticks to cook what I have for my son and me. After that, we will starve to death.' Elijah said, 'Everything will be fine.'

God had promised Elijah that if he went to Zarephath in Sidon, a widow there would look after him. It must have come as a bit of a shock to discover she was so poor that she had nothing to share. But God had told him and he clearly felt confident enough to insist she used up her last bit of flour and oil on him and to say that everything was going to be all right. And, of course, it was. The widow made Elijah a little loaf with all the ingredients she had and God made sure that she did not run out of food for a long time.

What do we do with a story like that? Our experience does not always mirror that of the widow. We do our best to share what we have and we run out! And then, just at the point when we feel the cupboard is bare and we have absolutely nothing to share, God asks us for more.

My mother-in law once found herself in exactly that position. She had bought two pieces of fish and dipped them in batter and was about to fry them for supper when her husband arrived with an unexpected guest. What did she do? Fry an extra bit of batter for herself and munch it with gusto, pretending it had fish inside! Problem solved.

Of course, sometimes it's not that simple. We run out of not only material goods but also energy, patience, goodwill and even faith. Then it is not so easy to cover it up. More and more I find myself saying, 'OK God. I'll try, but it's up to you. You've sent these people to me to help. Give me what it takes to do the job, 'cos I ain't got nothing left.' Almost always, everything turns out fine, just as it did for the widow of Sidon.

....

Help us to trust you even when what we encounter seems so far from what you appeared to promise.

BP

113

Safe from the world

A short time later Mary hurried to a town in the hill country of Judea. She went into Zechariah's home, where she greeted Elizabeth. When Elizabeth heard Mary's greeting, her baby moved within her... Mary stayed with Elizabeth about three months. Then she went back home.

And mustn't Elizabeth have been glad of the company! It must have been very quiet in Zechariah's house. Her husband had not been able to speak since he had been foolish enough to argue with the angel who brought him the good news that he and Elizabeth were going to have a child. The lopsided conversations of her saying something and him writing a reply must have been a strain for them, especially since we are told she had just spent five months at home, not leaving the house. And now here was Mary, her cousin, come to stay—someone she could chatter with to her heart's content. They had so much to share. Two miracle pregnancies. Two very special babies. Can you just picture them shut away from the inquisitive world outside, swapping stories?

Of course, there are going to be differences as well. In Elizabeth's case her pregnancy means that when she finally leaves the house people will stop looking down on her for the first time. No one will ever again be able to point their finger at her and suggest her inability to conceive is a sign that God is punishing her. In Mary's case it will be the opposite. People will despise this girl who has become pregnant out of marriage. At this stage Mary does not even know how Joseph is going to react to the news. But for a while they were safe.

There are times in most of our lives when we need to withdraw from the world; to hide away. To spend time with those who do not judge us but simply love and listen. We need to seize those opportunities and go to the home of someone who loves us a lot.

....

Dear Father, thank you for giving Mary this special time. Help us to identify who we can go to when life gets too tough, or how we can help when someone else needs a safe place.

BP

Watching in the wings

Mary... was at a wedding feast in the village of Cana in Galilee. Jesus and his disciples... were there. When the wine was all gone Mary said to Jesus, 'They don't have any more wine.'... There were six water jars... Each jar held about a hundred litres. Jesus told the servants to fill them to the top with water... He said, 'Now take some water and give it to the man in charge of the feast.'... the man in charge drank some... '... you have kept the best until last!'

So this is where Jesus chose to perform his first miracle—in the hall of a house in an obscure country town somewhere in the area of Galilee. Why? For starters, there were a lot of characteristics of many of his other miracles. There was very little razzamatazz. Someone was in need; it mattered to them; they came to Jesus. He responded and he responded generously. Did he really need to convert quite so many water jars into wine? The place must have been swimming in about 600 litres of alcohol! Did it really need to be a better quality than the wine they had been drinking? I think, too, it was an opportunity to impress on his new followers what an adventure travelling together would be.

There is a lot of fun in this miracle. I can just picture the rest of the servants standing outside the banquet hall with Jesus and the disciples, watching, as if from the wings, while the cup of ex-water was brought to the master of the feast. The sip. The pause. The delight when it was declared superb. How they must have hugged each other and laughed. And dipped their fingers into the jars to try it for themselves. And filled up pitcher after pitcher with the new wonder wine.

But can it really be that the first major miracle of the Son of God was witnessed by a handful of servants? Well, Jesus did say his time had not yet come for public displays of his godliness. And then we have a precedent, of course—with some shepherds on a hillside. God just doesn't see people as we do!

....

Have you ever been asked to do something that, on the face of it, appeared absurd?

BP

115

God of the ordinary

Jesus left the meeting place with James and John, and they went home with Simon and Andrew. When they got there, Jesus was told that Simon's mother-in-law was sick in bed with fever. Jesus went to her. He took hold of her hand and helped her up. The fever left her, and she served them a meal.

Such a lovely practical miracle—Simon's wife's mother must have been so upset not to be able to make her son's friends a meal. Now she could. But this is also another early private miracle. Not designed to impress the world, but purely to build up the disciples' trust that not only was this indeed the Son of God, but also about what sort of God this was. A God of the ordinary. A God who cared about the things we care about. A God who comes to us. Who takes our hand and helps us up. Who helps us to fulfil our role in society.

I love children's prayers so much. When they have been told their heavenly Father cares about all the little things that happen in their lives, they believe it. So God, listening in to the club for small children I help to run regularly, hears about the fish having a fungus, what they want for their birthday, whether or not they will be picked for the football team and the deaths of so many hamsters that I sometimes wonder if God wishes in retrospect he had designed them slightly differently—less lovable and with a longer lifespan!

We can lose so much of this confidence when we get older. Sadly, he doesn't always sort out our problems as neatly as he did that of Peter's mother-in-law and this inevitably raises questions in our minds. Does he really want to know about what is important to me? Surely it is too trivial. I think this episode shows he really does. Either that or Jesus was just very hungry and no one else could cook!

....

Dear Father, we so easily lose confidence in your love for us. Today help us to bring you all that is on our minds not just those things we consider worthy of your attention.

BP

Grandmas and mums have their uses!

I want to see you, because that will make me truly happy. I also remember the genuine faith of your mother Eunice. Your grandmother Lois had the same sort of faith, and I am sure that you have it as well.

Both in Acts and in his letter to Timothy, Paul refers to the faith of Timothy's mother and grandmother. Timothy was like a son to Paul, probably his favourite person and who does he give the credit to? Not himself. He does not talk about what he has done in Timothy's life, but he credits the two women who taught him to follow Jesus when he was a small boy.

It is so easy when we are stuck at home with small children to feel that the real Christian walk is something other people are doing. Especially when our children are at the age when we find it easiest to like them best when they are tucked up asleep.

This story should give us encouragement. The ritual of bedtime stories and little prayers may often feel less than spirit-filled, especially when you are longing to finally have a bit of time to yourself. Sorting out arguments fairly and trying to persuade your children that sharing is fun may feel a bit feeble in contrast with some of the accomplishments of God's heroes. But Timothy's mum and grandma receive high praise for their efforts by God's greatest evangelist, so take a bow all of you who have been involved in the Christian nurture of children. By that I mean so much more than just Bible teaching. If Christian nurture is not accompanied by unconditional love, it can inoculate a child against faith for life. It's a tough job parents are called to. Thank goodness we can turn to God for forgiveness when we fail.

....

How much influence did your mother and grandmother have on your life? Take your reaction to God.

Read Acts 16:1–5 for the story of how Paul met Timothy.

BP

Home privileges

[The elder brother said to his father] '… you have never even given me a little goat, so that I could give a dinner for my friends… His father replied, 'My son, you are always with me, and everything I have is yours.'

Many years ago both my husband and I worked residentially as social workers and lived on site. Our decision to find a house away from our place of work was based on an incident when a boy who Adrian was working closely with became insanely jealous of our eldest son, to the point that we actually witnessed him throw a jagged, open can directly at our five-year-old's face. What this poor lad couldn't stand was that, however close Adrian was to him, only his own little boy lived at home with him.

We so often feel sorry for the elder brother in the story of the prodigal son. We feel with him his fury that the brother who has given so much grief to his father should be greeted with the fatted calf, the rings and the party. What we sometimes overlook is that he had the privilege of living with this wonderful man all the time; he could have whatever he asked for.

Sometimes those of us who never really experienced an electrifying conversion can feel pretty jealous of the fuss being made of returning prodigals. We can feel bored and tired and neglected, almost wishing we had messed up more just to get the celebration when we came back home.

Those of us in that position need to remember we are the lucky ones. We, like Timothy, have never experienced what it is like to be far away from our natural home. We have been dwelling with God for more of our lives and therefore have had available to us for longer all the privileges that go with sonship (and daughtership). If it hasn't been much fun, then maybe, just maybe, that's our fault!

....

Dear Father, help us to be thankful that you are our Father and to live as though everyday is our party.

BP

Everyone liked them

Day after day they met together in the temple. They broke bread together in different homes and shared their food happily and freely, while praising God. Everyone liked them, and each day the Lord added to their group others who were being saved.

The thing that hit me when I read this was that 'everyone liked them'. They were fun to be with, just as Jesus had been fun to be with. Their home groups were fun places to be. Places where you felt accepted. Places where food was shared generously. These people had a reputation for loving each other. No wonder God added to their group. He must have felt he could entrust newly saved souls to such wholesome, hospitable and genuinely loving folk. But it is interesting to note they also met together every day in the temple. In other words, they were first worshipping God and then loving their neighbours. Sounds like that new commandment Jesus gave us really works. It also sounds as though the one spilled over into the other, unlike some home groups, which have dreary Bible studies, hushed prayer times and then come alive for the coffee and share what really matters!

What sort of homes do you feel most comfortable in? Having had children, I would probably say the ones where I feel that I could eat a digestive biscuit without panicking about crumbs. Having been to many Bible home groups, I would say I feel the most comfortable in the ones where I can say what I think and feel without risk of censure. Where I can voice my doubts without someone immediately feeling the need to trot out the party line. Where I know I will be accepted as myself, where I am right now. Where I actually feel people are pleased to see me.

Sometimes Christians feel they need to present a perfect image—an immaculate theology. Well, I need to feel I can drop a few spiritual crumbs occasionally, and I think most people feel the same.

Would God add newly saved Christians to your home group?

....

Dear Father, help me to open my doors generously and joyfully to whoever you bring my way. I am sorry for my grumbling.

Read John 13:34–35 to discover Jesus' new commandment.

BP

119

God be in our homes

She must also be well known for doing all sorts of good things, such as raising children, giving food to strangers, welcoming God's people into her home, helping people in need, and always making herself useful.

The widow Paul is describing is God's ideal homemaker. OK, making herself useful must involve quite a bit of housework, but not at the expense of spending time with her children, having people in to eat, and helping people in need. That amounts to pretty comprehensive hospitality, doesn't it? The fact that nowadays most of us have to add a full-time job to that agenda, stretches our abilities to reach this ideal just a bit. On the other hand, poverty is not knocking on our doors quite so overtly. Of course, at the time of Paul, there would have been huge numbers of needy, hungry neighbours right on your doorstep. Now many of us have to look a little further to give food to strangers and help the needy.

Over the last three years my husband Adrian and I have been blessed by getting involved with the work of World Vision and child sponsorship. We have learnt what it means to quite literally not know where your next meal is to come from, what neighbourliness costs. I know it probably sounds a bit silly, but when I look at the photos of the children we sponsor, I love the sense that they are in our home, part of us, borrowed for a few years while they are growing up. They may not be sitting round our table, but we are giving them a daily meal. They may not be sleeping under our roof, but we are giving them a blanket. It's not much, but it's something and I know that just as their pictures are in our home, so our pictures are in theirs—almost as if we lived next door.

....

Dear Father, help us to give—to sacrifice our routines, to give our time, to share what we have, to learn what being a homemaker should be.

BP

Foundations that will stand

I once read a visitors' book where a guest thanked the host 'for making an embassy of heaven'. That home was like an outpost of Jesus' heavenly home—a place where people could meet Jesus; where they could be refreshed and sent on their way encouraged. Whether your home is a room or a palace, it can still be a place where people meet Jesus as you minister to their needs.

Whatever your home is like, it will need firm foundations. As Jesus said, 'Everyone who hears these words of mine and puts them into practice is like a wise man who built his house on the rock. The rain came down, the streams rose, and the winds blew and beat against that house; yet it did not fall, because it had its foundation on the rock' (Matthew 7:24–25). The storms of life are not just a possibility, they are certain to come. That's when the foundations of our lives are put to the test. That's when I need to be secure in my identity as a child of God. Make this hymn your prayer:

Before the throne of God above
I have a strong and perfect plea.
A great high priest whose name is Love
Who ever lives and pleads for me.
My name is graven on His hands,
My name is written on His heart.
I know that while in Heaven He stands
No tongue can bid me thence depart.

Behold Him there the risen Lamb,
My perfect spotless righteousness,
The great unchangeable I AM,
King of glory and of grace,
One with Himself I cannot die.
My soul is purchased by His blood,
My life is hid with Christ on high,
With Christ my Saviour and my God!

Charitie Lees Bancroft (1841–1923)

The end of the story?

Then I saw a new heaven and a new earth, for the first heaven and the first earth had passed away, and there was no longer any sea. I saw the Holy City, the new Jerusalem, coming down out of heaven from God, prepared as a bride beautifully dressed for her husband.

If we needed a title for our last two weeks of daily readings this year it would be easy to choose something that refers to these chapters in Revelation as the end of the story. And finally, perhaps? After all, this is the closing scene of God's marvellous rescue plan. Revelation is the last book in the Bible, and we are given a stunning picture of a new heaven and new earth coming down like a final curtain. The new heaven completely replaces the old, and the new earth has, as its centrepiece, the divinely created new Jerusalem.

But why would God make everything new (Revelation 21:5) if this is just the glorious end? Quite simply because this isn't the end—it's just the beginning. The beginning of a new life enjoying a perfect relationship with our Father God. This new earth is still recognizable—as a heavenly one. It is only the sea, itself a symbol of separation, that is removed. This is the new earth and new heaven for which we have all been waiting.

C.S. Lewis describes this new beginning perfectly in his final Narnia story, *The Last Battle* (1956):

The things that began to happen were so great and beautiful that I cannot write them. And for us this is the end of all the stories, and we can truly say that they all lived happily ever after. But for them it was the beginning of the real story. All their life in this world and all their adventures in Narnia had only been the cover and the title page: now at last they were beginning Chapter One of the Great Story which no one on earth has read: which goes on for ever: in which every chapter is better than the one before.

....

Lord, as we contemplate the opening pages of a new story give us a glimpse of the new heaven that awaits us.

Read Isaiah 65:17–25 for a preview of the new story.

WB

What will the new heaven be like?

And he carried me away in the Spirit to a mountain great and high, and showed me the Holy City, Jerusalem, coming down out of heaven from God… and its brilliance was like that of a very precious jewel, like a jasper, clear as crystal.

While this picture is a preview of the new Jerusalem it gives us an indication of the unsurpassed and unimaginable beauty of all God has prepared for us in the new heaven. And it is just that—an indication. We simply haven't the ability to imagine something so wonderful. The descriptions of brilliance and the jewel-like comparisons enchant us. The vivid colours and breathtaking vistas may capture our imagination, but they can only give us a glimpse of all that our heavenly Father has prepared for us. Our limited language and logic prevent us from seeing what lies ahead. It is a mystery, a secret, a big surprise.

When I was a child I desperately wanted to know what was in those packages my mum thought she had hidden successfully away at the bottom of her wardrobe in readiness for Christmas! Yet I knew that if I did prod and poke, or even go as far as to open them a little and peep inside, the delight of Christmas morning would be taken away and the joy of anticipation would be deflated. I just had to imagine—and hope!

It really is the same with heaven. It's never a wise idea to poke and prod at what might be waiting for us. Even if we think we have successfully lifted the wrapping on all that awaits us, we will only get a glimpse. We can never know the extent of the joy and delight of heaven. We can't even begin to imagine it, because we don't understand the unfathomable depths of our need for heaven, let alone how that need will be met perfectly by our God.

As Joni Eareckson Tada says, 'We cannot conjure up heaven with our minds; our desires go deeper than what our minds imagine' (*What Will Heaven Be Like?*, Marshall Pickering, 1995).

....

'Heaven is peace dancing'
(G. K. Chesterton, The
Everlasting Man).

Read 1 Corinthians 2:9–10 for
more of God's secret.

WB

Investing in heaven

Set your hearts on things above, where Christ is seated at the right hand of God. Set your minds on things above, not on earthly things. For you died, and your life is now hidden with Christ in God. When Christ, who is your life, appears, then you also will appear with him in glory.

You will probably have seen the amusing bumper sticker that proclaims, 'Retired and happy—and spending our kids' inheritance!' It implies something of a second thought on the part of the parents in regard to their children. When we have a challenging day with our teenage daughter, my husband says he can understand the inclination—at least where any inheritance for her, if not her brother, is concerned. He wonders if it is worth investing anything in one who lives so much for the moment with very little thought for the future or for the one trying to secure it for her—at least financially!

Our inheritance in heaven is rather different, of course. It doesn't depend on the whims of a parent with a change of heart, but solely on the sacrifice made for us by Christ on the cross. He is the only reason we stand to inherit anything. It follows, then, that in gratitude for God's grace, our focus shouldn't be on all we can gain in this world, but on all we need to do to prepare for the next. This means shifting our focus and setting our minds on things above, on the heavenly things we can invest in now that will prepare us for our inheritance in heaven. That inheritance is assured but we can add value to our joy in its receipt by our added investments. We can do that by investing ahead in terms of service, obedience, love and a life lived for God, as an indication that we understand and appreciate what our inheritance means.

If we are to share a heavenly throne in the future with the one who, in saving us, gave us that privilege, we ought to spend time getting to know him and finding out how he would have us live now.

....

'Aim at heaven and you will get earth thrown in: aim at earth and you will get neither' (C.S. Lewis).

Read Revelation 3:14–22 to learn more about the heavenly perspective on poverty and riches.

WB

Waiting on tiptoe

The creation waits in eager expectation for the children of God to be revealed. For the creation was subjected to frustration... in hope that the creation itself will be liberated from its bondage to decay and be brought into the glorious freedom of the children of God.

'In eager expectation' is a perfect description of the way children wait for Christmas. In my Advent book, *The Art of Waiting* (BRF, 2004), I describe the lengths to which we went when our children were small to hasten the day they were waiting for. We would try to keep them busy, help them understand some of the real meaning of Christmas and do everything we could to focus on the joy of that day, but without hype. Nevertheless, they would almost be on tiptoe waiting for the next morning to reveal all they had been waiting for.

The world also waits on tiptoe in eager expectation for a promised special day: a day of liberation from decay, suffering and frustration. In this passage Paul uses our sufferings, and those of creation, to show a clear difference between what we know in this world and what we can expect in the next. As nature shares in that suffering, so it will share in the glory. Meanwhile—we wait.

The Greek word for 'eager expectation' (*apokaradokia*) gives us a beautiful picture of the way we should wait for heaven. It, too, indicates someone standing on tiptoe, looking straight at the horizon, straining to see whatever is coming. While we are waiting for our true identity as God's children to be revealed, creation also waits for that day because it will signal the renewal of earth and heaven, the moment when creation will also share in God's glory. That glory will be a fulfilment of all that God originally intended our humanity—and our home—to be.

We might ask ourselves two questions. Are we really waiting on tiptoe for God to reveal a new heaven and a new earth? And what should we be doing as we wait?

....

Let the anticipation and excitement of Christmas inspire you to stand on tiptoe in expectation of heaven.

Read 2 Timothy 4:7–8 for a glimpse of the crowning glory that awaits you on that day.

WB

Heavenly housework?

'Do not let your hearts be troubled. Trust in God; trust also in me. In my Father's house are many rooms: if it were not so, I would have told you. I am going there to prepare a place for you. And if I go and prepare a place for you, I will come back and take you to be with me that you also may be where I am.'

If you have guests staying for Christmas, you will doubtless be in the throes of making lists, vacuuming carpets and dusting rooms to prepare for their stay. In such a busy period, it's easy to have some elementary understanding of what Jesus means by his intention to prepare a place for the disciples, and ultimately, for us. But we mustn't become complacent about these verses, or limit their scope and tenderness by being content to leave our understanding at a level of cosy familiarity.

Look first at the context in which they were spoken: Jesus is about to face his own terrible death and separation from his Father. Yet he recognizes his friends' vulnerability in their imminent separation from him. He takes time to equip them for all that is ahead, and to comfort them with the assurance that they will one day be with him at home.

Jesus' reference to his Father's house underlines for us again the fabulous fact that heaven really is our home. A father's house may not be a welcoming picture for everyone, but this Father's house is an eternal refuge of gracious love and acceptance—and our place is already lovingly prepared. Whether or not there really are rooms in heaven is of little importance. Jesus' choice of words communicates a real sense of belonging, security and hope in heaven. It was just what the disciples needed to hear at this turbulent time.

We, too, will one day be with him in the place where we are loved children. Perhaps the disciples' bewildered words could be summed up as a child's cry of 'Are we nearly there yet?' 'Nearly,' says Jesus—'I'm just going ahead to get things ready.'

....

Whether or not you will welcome family home this Christmas, imagine the heavenly welcome home you will receive in the Father's house!

Read 2 Corinthians 5:1–5 for a heavenly perspective on our earthly home.

WB

An international celebration

After this I looked and there before me was a great multitude that no one could count, from every nation, tribe, people and language, standing before the throne and in front of the Lamb.

A few years ago I enjoyed a wonderful display of nativity crib scenes, many of which were collected by the journalist and broadcaster Libby Purvis. What fascinated me most was the way in which the country and culture of origin of each one created subtle differences and interpretations of the nativity scene. They reminded me, as I so often need to be reminded, that Christians all over the world celebrate the birth of Jesus alongside each other in very different circumstances of faith and fellowship. Yet we are all related through Jesus and his sacrifice for us on the cross.

The essence of heaven lies in relationship. Relationship to God and to Christ first and foremost, but also with the brothers and sisters who make up our wider family. Life in heaven will reflect that wonderful variety. It will not be an individual experience, but a family one, full of rich and fulfilling relationships. That relational dimension is one of the most precious elements in our hope of heaven. As family, we will share our life of love and service in perfect relationship with each other and with our God—without bickering or sibling rivalry!

In the New Testament, especially in Revelation, heaven is described as the great gathering of all the saints, a community of the redeemed and a reunion of all those who have believed in Jesus Christ. That great reunion will be so joyful and glorious it is compared to a wedding supper—perhaps the most familiar of joyful family occasions on earth. In this case it is the wedding banquet of the Lamb and we are invited! 'Then the angel said to me, "Write: blessed are those who are invited to the wedding supper of the lamb!"' (Revelation 19:9). What a wedding party that will be!

....

Pray for Christians celebrating Christmas in another country. How might you remember them amid the celebrations?

Read Revelation 5:10 to discover the special status of the community of the redeemed.

WB

127

Perfect joy

You have made known to me the path of life; you will fill me with joy in your presence, with eternal pleasures at your right hand.

If you cast your eye over your Christmas cards today, you will probably find one or two that wish you joy. The *New Penguin English Dictionary* defines joy as a feeling of great happiness, pleasure or delight; a source or cause of delight. It's a word that appears in the Bible hundreds of times. True joy has its origin and fulfilment in the work, promises and ultimately in the presence of God.

The writer of Hebrews tells us (12:2) that our race along the path of life ends in joy in heaven, and that we will be crowned with it. Jesus himself endured the cross because of the joy set before him. These different perspectives help us to understand that earthly joy is a pale imitation of the unique joy we'll know in heaven. Heavenly joy comes even from suffering. It is the result of dried tears and restored lives. The bliss of grace and the embrace of reunion.

The joy we will know then will be everywhere. The Bible says we will not only be crowned by it but overtaken by it (Isaiah 35:10). It will be over us, within us and all around us—even weighing us down from the top of our heads!

We mustn't think the pleasure referred to here is some kind of hedonistic trip. Pleasure will be found in our place at the right hand of God. There is no greater pleasure. All our earthly longings will be fulfilled in the heavenly joy of our relationship with him.

And of course, it is the same joy with which angels declared the birth of Jesus to shepherds thousands of years ago, with the words, 'I bring you good news of great joy!' (Luke 2:10). The work of salvation had begun—with great joy.

....

Write your own unique, personal definition of joy. Prop it up where you can see it and reflect on it over these special few days.

Read Psalm 96:11–13 for a picture of a joyful creation.

WB

True worship

How lovely is your dwelling-place, O Lord Almighty! My soul yearns, even faints, for the courts of the Lord… Blessed are those who dwell in your house; they are ever praising you.

Christmas Day, for most of us, is a day of coming together to celebrate the birth of Jesus. Often we are meeting up with friends and relations for the first time for a long time. There are hugs and exclamations of surprise. Children hear those familiar words, 'Haven't you grown?' and the joy we spoke about in yesterday's reading is almost tangible.

There is often a sparkle and youthful energy in our church worship on Christmas morning, which escapes us for the rest of the year! A carefree, uninhibited, childlike whoopee in response to the goodness of God. Perhaps it's something to do with the way in which children are central at Christmas—it *is* all about a baby!

Your home might be full of special people as you read these words. You might welcome loved ones later in the day, or join a celebration at the home of friends or relatives. Maybe you will hold tender memories of Christmases past close to your heart in quiet moments.

Our celebrations on this special day share some similarities with the worship in the house of the Lord described in this psalm. It is a dwelling-place of security and blessing where he is continually praised. It offers just a glimpse of what it will be like to live with God in his house and worship him together as his children. In heaven, we will take our place at the ultimate feast of celebration—the wedding feast of the Lamb—with an even greater multitude of spiritual friends and family. It will be the beginning of perfect celebratory worship that our earthly celebration today can only hint at. We will be able to worship God as he intended, in intimacy, face to face, because of Jesus—the gift of grace that he gave us on the first Christmas Day.

....

As you celebrate today, look at the faces of family and friends, or at photographs of previous celebrations, and anticipate the party that awaits you in heaven.

Read Revelation 19:6–8 for John's glimpse of that worshipping wedding party in heaven.

WB

All working perfectly

No longer will there be any curse. The throne of God and of the Lamb will be in the city, and his servants will serve him. They will see his face, and his name will be on their foreheads.

Today, I hope, we will be enjoying the relative relaxation of the Christmas break—once all the cooking is done! However, as I am often a restless, workaholic kind of creature, it isn't long before I am itching to be doing something. So I am always very relieved to know that heaven will be a busy place. The best thing about that busyness will be its purpose. David Winter assures us: 'We shall not sit on wispy clouds playing harps, but we shall have good useful, satisfying activity. We shall perfectly, at last, serve him' (*What Happens After Death*, Barbour Publishing, 2000).

I rather like that word 'perfectly'! It means that our work and service will not be subject to the usual delays and frustrations. We will not be all fingers and thumbs, run out of materials, get stuck or worry whether or not other people will keep their part of the bargain. We will be able to focus on the job in hand and do it perfectly. Engaging continuously in the worship of God, we will simultaneously carry out his will. This is a timely reminder that everything we do on earth should be considered worship; an imperfect apprenticeship for heaven.

The other wonderful thing is that in heaven God's will *will* be done. The agenda will be his and every item on it will be purposeful and fulfilling. No long meetings for meetings' sake, no committee decisions to stagger towards via argument and point-scoring. We will all be serving him in perfect agreement and unison. Neither will we feel unappreciated by, or distant from the boss.

God's name will be on our foreheads and we will see him as he is in a perfect working relationship. How could heaven be less than fulfilling when it follows such a glorious work ethic—and for the King of Heaven?

....

How does seeing the face of the one we love enable us to serve him better?

Read Matthew 6:9–10 to remind yourself how God's will has always been done in heaven.

WB

A heavenly body

So it will be with the resurrection of the dead. The body that is sown is perishable, it is raised imperishable; it is sown in dishonour, it is raised in glory; it is sown in weakness, it is raised in power; it is sown a natural body, it is raised a spiritual body.

The toll of everyday life and ageing inevitably lead us to comment: I could do with a new body! For two of my friends suffering chronic illness, that longing is particularly heartfelt. Neither can wait for that moment when their burdensome body will be transformed.

However, we will retain the essence of our personalities (just the positive traits, I hope!) because our uniqueness is precious to the creator God who formed each of us in our mother's womb (Psalm 139:13). The implication is that we will recognize each other. Can you imagine the wonder of that? What a comfort such assurance is to those of us whose loved ones have gone home ahead of us.

Although our heavenly bodies will still bear some resemblance to our earthly forms, they will not be wispy shadows of our former selves but strong, healthy and glorious. Joni Eareckson-Tada wrote about a dream she had in which her disabled body was transformed, in heaven, into one that swam across a pool with lithe and healthy limbs, just as she did as a young girl before the diving accident that left her a quadriplegic. Those limbs, she said, were golden and gleaming.

The truth is we will need new bodies in heaven, not just because the old ones will be worn out, but because they will be inadequate for heavenly life and incapable of living in the light of God's glory. Our glowing physique, free from the ravages of sickness and decay, ageing and infirmity, will be designed to fulfil all its new purposes in heaven, boldly declaring our heavenly origins as children of God.

Now that's what it really means to wear a designer label!

....

Augustine said, 'The rapture of the saved soul will flow over into the glorified body'. Meditate on what that might mean.

Read Philippians 3:20–21 to discover how the prospect of our heavenly bodies should energize us, now.

WB

No more suffering or death

But only the redeemed will walk there, and the ransomed of the Lord will return. They will enter Zion with singing; everlasting joy will crown their heads. Gladness and joy will overtake them, and sorrow and sighing will flee away.

'I dread Christmas,' I overheard an elderly woman say in the super-market. 'It brings everything back.' For many of us, Christmas brings sadness and grief or reminders of past Christmases that were far from merry. Suffering, pain and tears are a reality of life, even in a season traditionally marked by joy. Sometimes we feel as if we are bound by painful memories; we long for freedom.

This beautiful passage from Isaiah reminds us that for those whom God has redeemed there is hope—that whatever pain, separation, per-secution or suffering we may know in this life, there is a pathway that leads us back to security and joy and the safe eternal arms of the Father. The pilgrims here are returning to the place from which they were previously exiled. They are heading home, just as we are head-ing home to heaven. The promise of heaven is not pie in the sky when you die or even cake on a plate as you wait, but what Paul calls a firm and secure hope (Hebrews 6:19).

The most painful realities of this life will disappear. In Revelation 21:4 John mentions five examples: tears, death, mourning, crying and pain, but the list could be longer. All these terrible realities will disap-pear because Christ makes everything new (21:5). One day in heaven we will be free from even the memory of them—free to be daughters of our heavenly Father, living in the loving relationship he intended.

The epitaph for Martin Luther King, whose life was lost in the fight for freedom from racial hatred and persecution, reads: 'Martin Luther King 1929–1968. Free at last, free at last, Thank God Almighty I'm free at last.'

....

What do you long to be free of?   Read Revelation 21:4–5 as a
Share those longings with God   reminder that it is God himself
in prayer.   who will wipe our tears away.

                                                                    WB

Intimate relationship

Dear friends, now we are children of God, and what we will be has not yet been made known. But we know that when he appears, we shall be like him, for we shall see him as he is.

One of the conveniences I dislike most is the telephone. I know it's great for keeping in touch, and if it's a friend I know well on the other end, and we are catching up on chatty news, it's not so bad. But if there's something important to be said and heard I find it difficult. I don't like being unable to see the person I am listening and talking to. I feel as if I have an incomplete picture to interpret. We learn so much from the facial expressions and body language of another person, especially in conversation, that I find it almost impossible to do without those hidden forms of communication. The telephone doesn't seem to bring us closer together, it just creates a barrier.

I feel the same about my relationship with Jesus. It's so frustrating not being able to see him! I want to be able to talk to him face to face, to watch the expression in his eyes and the curl of amusement at the corners of his mouth. So I particularly long for the time when I will see him as he is. (I still find it quite difficult to accept that I will also be like him!)

In heaven our relationship with the Father and the Son will be transformed. It will not be handicapped by earthly barriers because heaven is primarily about relationship. The emphasis of life in heaven is relational not hedonistic. We are to be with Jesus and like him, fully seen and fully known. Our relationship with him will—at last—be a face-to-face relationship, with no interference!

C.S. Lewis writes: 'We shall have turned… from the portraits to the original from the rivulets to the fountain, from the creatures he made lovable to love himself…' (*The Four Loves*, Fount, 2002).

....

Face to face with Jesus. What does that mean to you? How might you live with such an awe-inspiring prospect?

Read 1 Corinthians 13:12 for a clearer picture of just how we will be seen and known in heaven.

WB

Everlasting relationship

And I heard a loud voice from the throne saying, 'Now the dwelling of God is with human beings, and he will live with them. They will be his people, and God himself will be with them and be their God...'

We have returned to this beautiful passage from Revelation 21 to focus on verses 3–4, which promise us that in heaven the dwelling of God is with human beings. There can't be anything much more wonderful than contemplating living with someone who loves us very much and whom we adore.

One of my dearest young friends has recently fallen in love. Yes, it's all very sweet. But this is a very new and different relationship for her, as it is the first romantic partnership she has entered into since becoming a Christian. Suddenly there are clear boundaries for sharing her life with another in loving relationship. He is a Christian too, with a prominent position in church life, just as smitten and, she admits, it's difficult! They want to be together, live together in the same place, all the time, day and night. But, of course, for most Christians the understanding is that doing so before marriage would not be God's way. That's so tough for them! But they know that one day they will reach the point where marriage will allow them to unreservedly commit themselves to each other and enjoy life together to the full.

Yet their idea of bliss is a pale comparison of what it will be like for God to live with us. While we live in a world so imperfect and bound by sin, it is almost impossible to understand how wonderful that will be.

Amazingly it is death itself—no longer to be feared—that will enable us to live in such close relationship. Alister McGrath writes: 'Indeed death merely snaps the final surly bonds which link us with the unredeemed world of sin, enabling us to commit ourselves totally and unreservedly to Christ' (*Why Does God Allow Suffering?*, Hodder & Stoughton, 2000).

....

Meditate on these words of Jesus: 'and then after a little while you will see me' (John 16:16).

Read Psalm 17:15 to reflect further on that first moment of intimacy with Jesus.

WB

Everlasting security

For I am convinced that neither death nor life, neither angels nor demons, neither the present nor the future, nor any powers, neither height nor depth, nor anything else in all creation, will be able to separate us from the love of God that is in Christ Jesus our Lord.

Today is New Year's Eve. You might be planning to attend a Watchnight church service, or a thanksgiving celebration. Or perhaps you will send off the old year and welcome in 2006 in party style.

Whatever you choose to do to mark the turning of the year, you will doubtless experience that unfathomable mix of celebration and regret, apprehension and hope that New Year's Eve often brings.

As Christians we know we can trust our God for tomorrow, whatever it might contain. But that isn't always easy. Most of us like to know what we are doing in advance and will buy new diaries, calendars and organizers ready to fill in our appointments and plans. Yet we can never really know what the future holds, whether that future is tomorrow, next week or next year, let alone our future in eternity. But if we are trusting the God who holds the past and future in his hands and who is Alpha and Omega, the beginning and the end, do we really need to know?

When my children were young they were so frustrated if they asked a question like 'What's for tea?' or 'Where are we going?', and I answered, 'Wait and see!' Despite their love of surprises, something deep inside them really just wanted to know. Few of us like uncertainty—even when it is implied by a parent or someone else we love and trust. It's the same with our hope of heaven and all the eternal wonders it promises. We'd really like to know.

Dr John Polkinghorne, the mathematician and priest, was asked, 'What will life be like after death?' He replied: 'Well, we shall have to wait and see.' That really should be a perfectly acceptable answer to those who are God's children and trust him with their heavenly future.

....

We do not know what the future holds, but we know who holds the future.

Read Revelation 22:12 for Jesus' promise of heavenly certainties.

WB

Drawn into intimacy with God

John's vision of heaven in Revelation reminds us that God is drawing us into the future he has prepared for us. Ever since Adam and Eve were banished from Eden, humanity has been longing for the intimacy with God and that home we have lost, along with his presence, protection and abundant provision.

In Egypt, the children of Israel longed for freedom; in the desert, they longed for the promised land. Today, people are still longing for the intimacy of God's presence—though few can interpret those longings. Fortunately, God takes the initiative. He is always speaking; drawing us into that intimacy, if we can only see and hear. As Michael Mitton writes in *A Heart to Listen* (BRF, 2004), p. 110:

'Despite the materialism of our Western world, our longing for paradise will never be eliminated. Humans cannot live on the bread of this world alone. We all need the bread of heaven as we journey as pilgrims through an often barren land. God has put an amazing ability in our hearts to become conscious of the things of heaven. He has created windows in our souls that can open to see new views that can transform our lives. Like Moses, at any moment we may discover the extraordinary in the ordinary. Is this not one of the gifts that Christian people can offer to our world? We can be those who show that there is another world, not a million miles from this one. There is a kingdom of heaven that touches every part of this fragile earth. Everything in this earth can be touched by God to speak of things eternal. Part of our calling is to listen to others in such a way as to help them discover their own longings to touch heaven.'

As you reflect on this series of Bible readings, ask God to open your eyes and ears to see his rescue plan in action in your life and the lives of others. Invite him to use you and your home to reach others. Expect surprises as he draws you deeper into the wonderful adventure of life in Christ.

Try Hebrews!

The New Testament book of Hebrews is one of my personal favourites. It helps me to see the big picture of what God has been doing to set his rescue plan in motion, as it helps to explain the Old Testament images of priests, covenant, the tabernacle, the temple and sacrifice which all point forward to Jesus.

But it's not simply an exercise in religious symbolism. It has practical implications. Like so many New Testament letters, after a long introduction and explanation, it turns on the word 'therefore' (10:19). 'Therefore' because God has fleshed out all the Old Testament symbols and pictures in his Son Jesus, 'since we have confidence to enter the Most Holy Place by the blood of Jesus, by a new and living way opened for us through the curtain, that is, his body, and since we have a great priest over the house of God, let us draw near to God with a sincere heart in full assurance of faith...'

The writer says 'let us' five times in four short verses. I always think of them as the Hebrew lettuces: 'let us draw near to God... Let us hold unswervingly to the hope we profess... let us consider how we may spur one another on toward love and good deeds... Let us not give up meeting together... let us encourage one another' (10:23–25).

If you'd like to invest some time studying Hebrews, why not use BRF's *People's Bible Commentary* series to get started? Dick France, author of the commentary on Hebrews, says in his overview of the book:

'There was a popular song many years ago which had the refrain "Anything you can do, I can do better." For "you" put the religion of the Old Testament, and for "I" put Christ, and you have an excellent summary of what Hebrews is all about.'

Other Christina Press titles

Who'd Plant a Church? Diana Archer (£5.99)

Planting an Anglican church from scratch, with a team of four—two adults and two children—is an unusual adventure even in these days. Diana Archer gives a distinctive perspective on parish life.

Pathway Through Grief edited by Jean Watson (£6.99)

Ten Christians, each bereaved, share their experience of loss. Frank and sensitive accounts offering comfort and reassurance to those recently bereaved and new insights to those involved in counselling.

God's Catalyst Rosemary Green (£8.99)

Insight, inspiration and advice for both counsellors and concerned Christians who long to be channels of God's Spirit to help those in need. A unique tool for the non-specialist counsellor.

Angels Keep Watch Carol Hathorne (£5.99)

After 40 years, Carol Hathorne obeyed God's call to Kenya. She came face to face with dangers, hardships and poverty, but experienced the joy of learning that Christianity is still growing in God's world.

Not a Super-Saint Liz Hansford (£6.99)

Describes the outlandish situations that arise in the Manse, where life is both fraught and tremendous fun. A book for the ordinary Christian who feels they must be the only one who hasn't quite got it together.

The Addiction of a Busy Life Edward England (£5.99)

Twelve lessons from a devastating heart attack. Edward, a giant of Christian publishing in the UK, and founder of Christina Press, shares what the Lord taught him when his life nearly came to an abrupt end.

Life Path Luci Shaw (£5.99)

Keeping a journal can enrich life as we live it, and bring it all back later. Luci Shaw shows how a journal can also help us grow in our walk with God.

Precious to God Sarah Bowen (£5.99)

Two young people have their expectations shattered by the birth of a handicapped child. What was initially a tragedy is, through faith, transformed into a story of inspiration, hope and spiritual enrichment.

Other BRF titles

Women of the Word ed. Jackie Stead (£6.99)

This collection of Bible studies, written by a group of women writers, focuses on the lives of a host of female characters from Old and New Testaments, including Esther, Abigail, Lydia and others whom the Bible does not even name. First published in *Woman Alive* magazine as part of the 'Good Foundations' series, the studies show how these women can reach down the centuries and speak into our lives today.

A Heart to Listen Michael Mitton (£7.99)

This accessible book shows how, with God's help, we can relearn the art of listening and in doing so become a source of help and healing for others and for ourselves. Biblical reflection is interwoven with insights from the author's wide experience of listening ministry in the UK and abroad. Between chapters are episodes of an intriguing story, which explores the book's themes through vividly imagined characters in a cross-cultural setting.

Walking with Jesus through Advent and Christmas Murray McBride (£9.99)

This 'visual pilgrimage' has been created to provide a biblical 'story-map', designed as a way for the whole family, individuals, church-based children's groups or schools to prepare for Christmas. The material guides you through the Christmas narrative by using imaginative footprint illustrations. The footprints can be coloured and cut out to make your own frieze at home, or photocopied to use with groups, and made into a long Advent frieze to hang on the wall or unfold on the floor.

PBC Timothy, Titus and Hebrews Dick France (£7.99)

The People's Bible Commentary (PBC) series is designed for all those who want to study the scriptures in a way that will warm the heart as well as instruct the mind. This volume offers commentary on Paul's pastoral letters and on the letter to the Hebrews, with its compelling presentation of how, in the coming of Jesus, God has given us something 'better' than all that had gone before in the Old Testament period.

YOU CAN ORDER THE TITLES ON THESE TWO PAGES FROM CHRISTINA PRESS OR BRF, USING THE ORDER FORMS ON PAGES 140 AND 141.

Christina Press Publications Order Form

All of these publications are available from Christian bookshops everywhere or, in case of difficulty, direct from the publisher. Please make your selection below, complete the payment details and send your order with payment as appropriate to:

Christina Press Ltd, 17 Church Road, Tunbridge Wells, Kent TN1 1LG

		Qty	Price	Total
8700	God's Catalyst	____	£8.99	____
8702	Precious to God	____	£5.99	____
8703	Angels Keep Watch	____	£5.99	____
8704	Life Path	____	£5.99	____
8705	Pathway Through Grief	____	£6.99	____
8706	Who'd Plant a Church?	____	£5.99	____
8708	Not a Super-Saint	____	£6.99	____
8705	The Addiction of a Busy Life	____	£5.99	____

POSTAGE AND PACKING CHARGES				
	UK	Europe	Surface	Air Mail
£7.00 & under	£1.25	£2.25	£2.25	£3.50
£7.10–£29.99	£2.25	£5.50	£7.50	£11.00
£30.00 & over	free	prices on request		

Total cost of books £ _____
Postage and Packing £ _____
TOTAL £ _____

All prices are correct at time of going to press, are subject to the prevailing rate of VAT and may be subject to change without prior warning.

Name _____

Address _____

_____

_____ Postcode _____

Total enclosed £ _____ (cheques should be made payable to 'Christina Press Ltd')

[ ] Please do not send me further information about Christina Press publications

BRF Publications Order Form

All of these publications are available from Christian bookshops everywhere, or in case of difficulty direct from the publisher. Please make your selection below, complete the payment details and send your order with payment as appropriate to:

BRF, First Floor, Elsfield Hall, 15–17 Elsfield Way, Oxford OX2 8FG

		Qty	Price	Total
425 7	Women of the Word	____	£6.99	____
269 6	A Heart to Listen	____	£7.99	____
360 9	Walking with Jesus through Advent and Christmas	____	£9.99	____
119 3	PBC Timothy, Titus and Hebrews	____	£7.99	____

POSTAGE AND PACKING CHARGES				
	UK	Europe	Surface	Air Mail
£7.00 & under	£1.25	£3.00	£3.50	£5.50
£7.10–£29.99	£2.25	£5.50	£6.50	£10.00
£30.00 & over	free	prices on request		

Total cost of books £ _____
Postage and Packing £ _____
TOTAL   £ _____

All prices are correct at time of going to press, are subject to the prevailing rate of VAT and may be subject to change without prior warning.

Name _____

Address _____

_____

_____ Postcode _____

Total enclosed £ _____ (cheques should be made payable to 'BRF')
Payment by: cheque ❑ postal order ❑ Visa ❑ Mastercard ❑ Switch ❑

Card no. | | | | | | | | | | | | | | | | | |

Card expiry date | | | | Issue number (Switch) | | | |

Signature _____
(essential if paying by credit/Switch card)

❑ Please do not send me further information about BRF publications

Visit the BRF website at www.brf.org.uk

DBDWG0305   BRF is a Registered Charity

Subscription Information

Each issue of *Day by Day with God* is available from Christian book-shops everywhere. Copies may also be available through your church Book Agent or from the person who distributes Bible reading notes in your church.

Alternatively you may obtain *Day by Day with God* on subscription direct from the publishers. There are two kinds of subscription:

Individual Subscriptions are for four copies or less, and include postage and packing. To order an annual Individual Subscription please complete the details on page 144 and send the coupon with payment to BRF in Oxford. You can also use the form to order a Gift Subscription for a friend.

Church Subscriptions are for five copies or more, sent to one address, and are supplied post free. Church Subscriptions run from 1 May to 30 April each year and are invoiced annually. To order a Church Subscription please complete the details opposite and send the coupon to BRF in Oxford. You will receive an invoice with the first issue of notes.

All subscription enquiries should be directed to:

BRF
First Floor
Elsfield Hall
15–17 Elsfield Way
Oxford
OX2 8FG

Tel: 01865 319700
Fax: 01865 319701
E-mail: subscriptions@brf.org.uk

Church Subscriptions

The Church Subscription rate for *Day by Day with God* will be £10.50 per person until April 2006.

❑ I would like to take out a church subscription for _____ (Qty) copies.

❑ Please start my order with the January / April / September 2006* issue.
I would like to pay annually/receive an invoice with each edition of the notes*.
(*Please delete as appropriate)

Please do not send any money with your order. Send your order to BRF and we will send you an invoice. The Church Subscription year is from May to April. If you start subscribing in the middle of a subscription year we will invoice you for the remaining number of issues left in that year.

Name and address of the person organising the Church Subscription:

Name _____

Address _____

_____

Postcode _____ Telephone _____

Church _____

Name of Minister _____

Name and address of the person paying the invoice if the invoice needs to be sent directly to them:

Name _____

Address _____

_____

Postcode _____ Telephone _____

Please send your coupon to:

BRF
First Floor
Elsfield Hall
15–17 Elsfield Way
Oxford
OX2 8FG

❑ Please do not send me further information about BRF publications

Individual Subscriptions

❏ I would like to give a gift subscription (please complete both name and address sections below)

❏ I would like to take out a subscription myself (complete name and address details only once)

The completed coupon should be sent with appropriate payment to BRF. Alternatively, please write to us quoting your name, address, the subscription you would like for either yourself or a friend (with their name and address), the start date and credit card number, expiry date and signature if paying by credit card.

Gift subscription name ————————————————————

Gift subscription address ———————————————————

————————————————————— Postcode —————

Please send to the above for one year, beginning with the January / May / September 2006 issue: (delete as applicable)

	UK	Surface	Air Mail
Day by Day with God	❏ £12.45	❏ £13.80	❏ £16.05
2-year subscription	❏ £21.90	N/A	N/A

Please complete the payment details below and send your coupon, with appropriate payment, to BRF, First Floor, Elsfield Hall, 15–17 Elsfield Way, Oxford OX2 8FG

Your name ——————————————————————————

Your address —————————————————————————

————————————————————— Postcode —————

Total enclosed £ _____ (cheques should be made payable to 'BRF')
Payment by: cheque ❏ postal order ❏ Visa ❏ Mastercard ❏ Switch ❏

Card no. | | | | | | | | | | | | | | | | | | |

Card expiry date | | | | | Issue number (Switch) | | | | |

Signature ——————————————————————————
(essential if paying by credit/Switch card)

NB: These notes are also available from Christian bookshops everywhere.

❏ Please do not send me further information about BRF publications